KRIEGSMARINE NORTH SEA COMMAND 1939–42

Germany's coastal naval campaign

Lawrence Paterson
Illustrated by Edouard A. Groult

OSPREY PUBLISHING
Bloomsbury Publishing Plc
Kemp House, Chawley Park, Cumnor Hill, Oxford OX2 9PH, UK
Bloomsbury Publishing Ireland Limited,
29 Earlsfort Terrace, Dublin 2, D02 AY28, Ireland
1385 Broadway, 5th Floor, New York, NY 10018, USA
E-mail: info@ospreypublishing.com
www.ospreypublishing.com

OSPREY is a trademark of Osprey Publishing Ltd

First published in Great Britain in 2025

© Osprey Publishing Ltd, 2025

All rights reserved. No part of this publication may be: i) reproduced or transmitted in any form, electronic or mechanical, including photocopying, recording or by means of any information storage or retrieval system without prior permission in writing from the publishers; or ii) used or reproduced in any way for the training, development or operation of artificial intelligence (AI) technologies, including generative AI technologies. The rights holders expressly reserve this publication from the text and data mining exception as per Article 4(3) of the Digital Single Market Directive (EU) 2019/790.

A catalogue record for this book is available from the British Library.

ISBN: PB 9781472867438; eBook: 9781472867407; ePDF: 9781472867414; XML: 9781472867421

25 26 27 28 29 10 9 8 7 6 5 4 3 2 1

Maps by www.bounford.com
Diagrams by Adam Tooby
Battlescenes by Edouard A. Groult
Index by Mark Swift
Typeset by MPS Limited
Printed and bound in India by Repro India Ltd

Osprey Publishing supports the Woodland Trust, the UK's leading woodland conservation charity.

To find out more about our authors and books visit www.ospreypublishing.com. Here you will find extracts, author interviews, details of forthcoming events and the option to sign up for our newsletter.

For product safety related questions contact productsafety@bloomsbury.com

CONTENTS

THE FLEET'S PURPOSE	4
FLEET FIGHTING POWER	11
The Ships	
Technical Factors	
HOW THE FLEET OPERATED	34
Organization	
Command	
Intelligence	
Logistics and Facilities	
COMBAT AND ANALYSIS	48
The Fleet in Combat	
Analysis	
FURTHER READING	79
INDEX	80

THE FLEET'S PURPOSE

The North Sea was the earliest focal point of German naval operations during World War II. The European naval conflict of this period focuses predominantly on the Atlantic, as this is where the struggle over Britain's convoy lifelines took place. The Atlantic was arguably the key to Britain's survival. However, it was not Germany's. The German Atlantic war was offensive, not defensive, and in many ways the battles within the North Sea were of greater strategic importance to Germany, certainly in a defensive sense. Not only was the North Sea vital to the nautical transport of Germany's Norwegian mineral imports, in particular the iron ore shipments from Sweden's Gällivare and Kiruna mines, but this expanse of water also held the keys to the Atlantic Ocean and the Baltic Sea. Connecting to the Atlantic Ocean through the English Channel in the south and the Denmark Strait and Norwegian Sea in the north, the North Sea provided the only avenue by which Kriegsmarine units could take the war to the Atlantic convoys. The Baltic also represented trade routes with Scandinavia, the Baltic States and the Soviet Union; secure training grounds for German naval units; and a lifeline to the isolated land of the enclave of East Prussia, which had been separated from mainland Germany since 1918 by the Danzig Corridor. Furthermore, strategic German thinking of the 1920s had leaned towards Poland and France being the most likely adversaries in the event of future conflict, confirming how crucial a strong naval presence and at least partial control of the North Sea was to Germany.

However, by 25 August 1939 and the final moments before *Fall Weiss* (Plan White) and the attack on Poland, all Kriegsmarine operational plans were considered in compliance with the instructions issued by OKW (*Oberkommando der Wehrmacht*, Armed Forces High Command), according to which an extension of the conflict to the west was considered unlikely and all forces of the Navy were instead being concentrated in the east. In the west only unobtrusive security measures using U-boats and Luftwaffe maritime formations were being planned.

Kriegsmarine High Command had not envisioned how substantial the task of protecting German merchant shipping would be within the North Sea, as Britain would easily throttle all North Sea communications routes due to its naval strength and favourable geographic and military position. It would be impossible to maintain an open route militarily through the northern approaches to the North Sea for Germany's own supply routes, and only a small amount of shipping could traverse Norwegian and Danish territorial waters as a matter of survival travelling this route. However, the compulsory abandonment of the North Sea supply route would make greater forces available for offensive action against the enemy's supply lines. *Oberkommando der Kriegsmarine* (OKM) therefore decreed that the initial aim of naval warfare in the West was to cripple Britain's and France's military and economic imports by water.

(Left to right) Joseph Goebbels (Propaganda Minister), *Generaloberst* Werner von Blomberg (Minister of Defence), *Grossadmiral* Erich Raeder (head of the Kriegsmarine) and Adolf Hitler aboard the *Panzerschiff Deutschland* in April 1934. Hitler had an encyclopaedic knowledge of naval statistics but never fully understood the Navy's strategic role or methods. (Zume Press inc. / Alamy Stock Photo)

> The general tasks of the German Navy in wartime are:
> a. Protection of the coast against enemy operations from the sea and air;
> b. Protection of our own sea communications;
> c. Attack on enemy sea communications;
> d. Support of land and air warfare along the coast;
> e. Use as politico-strategic instrument of war, e.g., to ensure the neutrality of the Scandinavian countries and of the Baltic States.[1]

It was reckoned that Britain would endeavour to block the North Sea completely and thereby neutralize German bases and strongholds from carrying on the war in the Atlantic. The initial means would no doubt be the formation of a wide blockade; a tight costal blockade was unlikely due to the strength of German coastal defences including soon-to-be-laid minefields. Rather, it was assumed that the Royal Navy would limit its activities in the southern area of the North Sea to mine and submarine warfare, taking up cordon positions in the Channel and in the area between the Orkneys, Shetlands and Norway. If history repeated itself, the English Channel would soon become unnavigable by German military vessels and therefore the northern area of the North Sea was regarded from the very first as a focal point of the war at sea.

With that in mind, Raeder declared that the principal aims within that area were the constant disturbance of British operations and their establishment of an effective blockade, assisting the war in the Atlantic Ocean by tying up as

---
1 Battle Instructions for the Navy, May 1939.

many of the enemy forces as possible within home waters and the occasional brief opening of the British blockade for Atlantic combat forces returning to port or putting to sea. Not expecting to establish permanent mastery of the sea in this area, the Kriegsmarine instead would solve these problems by means of intensive small-scale warfare, surprise attacks on weaker units and a resultant accumulation of 'partial successes' and constant harassing action. In effect, theirs was to be nautical guerilla warfare.

In May 1939 the North Sea forces allocated to *Marinegruppenkommando West* amounted to:

Battleships *Gneisenau* (Flagship) and *Scharnhorst*;

Heavy cruiser *Admiral Hipper*;

Light cruiser *Leipzig*;

Destroyer Z1 *Leberecht Maass* (F.d.T. flagship);

2nd Destroyer Flotilla (2nd and 4th Destroyer Div.);

4th Destroyer Flotilla (6th and 8th Destroyer Div.);

6th Torpedo Boat Flotilla;

2nd S-boat Flotilla;

1st U-boat Flotilla (Type IIB, 9 boats);

2nd Minesweeping Flotilla;

2nd R-boat Flotilla;

Escort Flotilla.

During World War I, the largest naval battle and only full-scale engagement between battleships took place in the North Sea off the Danish Jutland peninsula. There, the Imperial German and Royal Navies fought an inconclusive battle at the end of May 1916 and, although Britain lost more ships and over twice as many men, Germany's High Seas Fleet never again sailed in force and access to the Atlantic Ocean and freedom of movement within the North Sea was denied. Thereafter, German naval hopes remained tied to the unrestricted U-boat campaign.

However, German supremacy within the North Sea during World War II was not a purely defensive issue. It provided opportunity to attack the Royal Navy's Home Fleet if circumstances allowed; not through the main battle fleet approach that had resulted in the Jutland battle of 1916, but rather the leeching effect of combined Luftwaffe maritime operations, S-boat operations and U-boat warfare. From the first day of the conflict with Britain, Admiral Sir Charles Forbes took elements of the Home Fleet on 'offensive sweeps' into the North Sea in an ineffectual attempt to show willing solidarity with Poland's distant struggle. Once Churchill insisted his perpetually offensive leanings were heard, so-called 'Units of Search' were formed that were centred on a cruiser or aircraft carrier to seek out enemy surface raiders or U-boats making for the North Atlantic. The destruction of carrier HMS *Courageous* on 17 September and several near misses on HMS *Ark Royal* soon ended this folly. Combined with minelaying successes against Royal Navy forces during the war's early weeks, Hitler was buoyant enough to relate in a speech given in the Reichs Chancellery to 200 assembled Wehrmacht officers on 23 November that, 'We have succeeded with our small navy in clearing the North Sea of the British.' He was, of course, mistaken.

The light cruiser *Leipzig*. The crane for the onboard Heinkel He 60 aircraft is a distinctive feature of the ship. *Leipzig* was severely damaged by submarine attack in December 1939 and never returned to fully operational service. (Author's collection)

Additionally, one of the Germans' primary offensive targets was the busy coastal convoy route that stretched between the Thames and the Firth of Forth that operated six days out of every seven, its most essential cargo being coal. London alone needed 40,000 tons per week to function. Britain's wartime economy could quite conceivably have been severely impacted, which could have led to partial or total collapse. The British North Sea coast is shallow and therefore vulnerable to minelaying. With German naval and Luftwaffe bases relatively close, this merchant traffic artery was at great risk.

Although there was little doubt that interdiction of the British Atlantic convoy routes remained the primary objective of the Kriegsmarine once war had been declared in 1939, it was not equipped to deliver a decisive blow. The end of World War I had seen the Imperial German Navy wracked with revolutionary chaos and the harsh terms of the Versailles Treaty limited the renamed Reichsmarine to a total of 15,000 men; Article 181 specified that Germany could not possess any U-boats and a commissioned surface fleet would be limited to six pre-dreadnought battleships, six light cruisers, 12 destroyers and 12 torpedo boats. Minesweepers were not under such restrictions, and Germany had been tasked with sweeping the extensive fields that its navy had laid during the war.

With a weak navy, Germany invested great effort into the development of mine warfare, eventually accumulating a range of magnetic, acoustic and pressure mines, as well as myriad timing devices by which mines could be triggered by the lead ship of a coastal convoy but detonate once the main body was likely to be overhead. Correspondingly, Germany's shallow North Sea coastline was perfect for enemy minelaying and, as much time and effort as the Reichsmarine and then Kriegsmarine spent in the development of the naval mine was equalled by its minesweeping capabilities. The North Sea would come to be a major minelaying battleground almost from the moment war was declared.

From September 1939, destroyers, torpedo boats and minelayers in company with light cruisers not only defensively mined the German Bight from the Dutch coast to the Skagerrak, but also laid extensive barrages close inshore along the British east coast, suffering casualties at the hands of the Royal Navy and, in one disastrous mistake, the Luftwaffe. This latter accident illustrates that the tumultuous relationship between the upper echelons of the Kriegsmarine and the Luftwaffe was never more difficult than during the struggle for control of the *Küstenflieger* (the German Naval Air Service) that operated maritime strike aircraft within the North Sea.

Germany continued to target the east-coast convoy routes bringing coal to London. A primary German target was the busy coastal convoy route that stretched between the Thames and Firth of Forth. Great Britain possessed a proportionately high coastline to land mass and the resources of the nation – coal being of the highest importance – were predominantly found in the less populated north but of greatest demand in the densely populated high consumption areas in the south, particularly London. This precious commodity was also required to fuel the industry and power stations of the south, and so the FN (northbound) and FS (southbound) convoy routes were established between the Thames and the Firth of Forth. Furthermore, the coastal convoy system that trailed through the North Sea eased the burden already placed on British west coast ports engaged in transatlantic trade, as well as relieving pressure on an overworked rail network by the facilitation of west to east movement of cargoes transhipped from larger vessels that had crossed the North Atlantic. This transference of cargoes from the large ocean-going merchants to smaller coastal steamers was often done in smaller subsidiary harbours, also alleviating congestion in Britain's main west coast ports. Indeed, by September 1940 when the Luftwaffe switched its bombers' attention to the capital, the larger ocean-going ships were barred from entering the Port of London until January 1941.

FRENCH CHANNEL COAST: GERMAN NAVAL ARTILLERY BATTERIES AND CONVOY ROUTES

The installation of heavy coastal artillery in the Pas de Calais region was undertaken almost immediately following the German occupation. Both naval and army batteries were ordered into position, the former into concrete installations while the latter comprised an assortment of impressive railway guns, some of which had been in action against the Maginot Line. Though originally envisioned as supporting guns for the proposed invasion of Britain – Operation *Seelöwe* (Sealion) – their effective purpose was the disruption of British coastal convoys. For this, the naval guns were well suited, while the railway guns brought to the area less so, as they possessed a limited and cumbersome traverse that required either the correctly curved piece of track or one of the turntables installed by the Wehrmacht for this purpose. When not firing, the railway guns were housed in reinforced concrete shelters known as *Dombunkers* due to their arched roof or by using existing railway buildings. Ultimately, the railway guns were used to bombard Dover and British coastal guns. The naval batteries had a hugely negative effect on the merchant seamen who manned the Channel convoys, but in actual fact sank only two ships through the entire war – both in June 1944 – damaging several more and killing two seamen.

As well as being used to disrupt British convoys, they, and subsequent smaller-calibre batteries later installed as part of the ambitious Atlantic Wall, were able to provide a degree of covering fire to German coastal convoys carrying supplies westward. Protected by defensive mine barriers, they came under increasing British aerial and naval pressure as the tide of war swung against Germany, with numerical and technological advantages becoming progressively the domain of Allies.

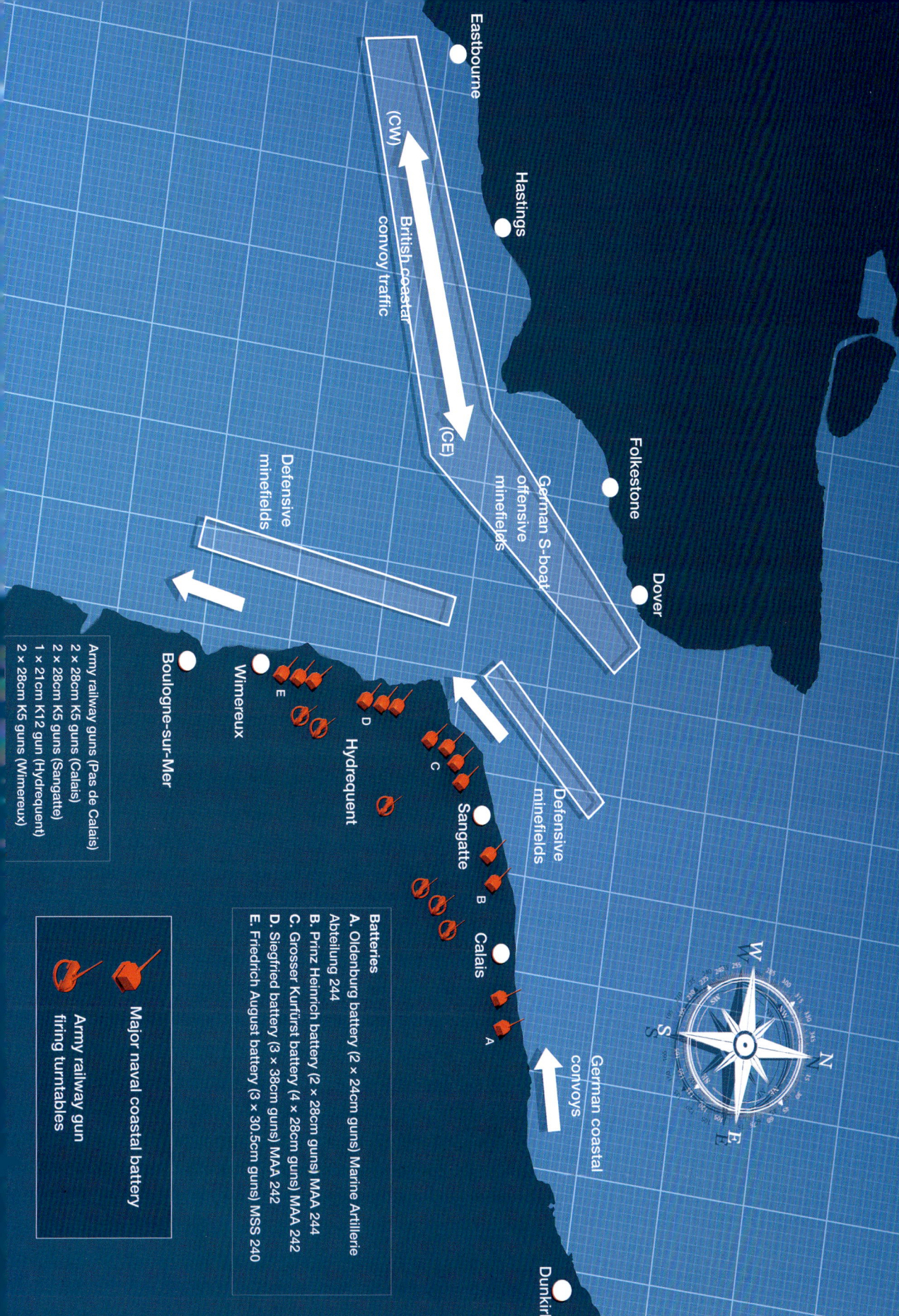

The quantity of merchant shipping engaged in this convoy traffic is frequently underestimated. Before the war, in 1937, 1,479 steam and motor vessels totalling 1,151,880 GRT and employing 21,324 British and 261 foreign seamen were primarily engaged along British coastal trade routes. British defensive convoying on the coastal routes was introduced in 1939, but following the fall of Scandinavia and France, the Kriegsmarine was able to establish naval installations that ranged from Norway's northern tip to the Franco–Spanish border. Short-range coastal attack vessels were better positioned to interdict coastal merchant traffic, for the first time posing a direct threat to traffic within the English Channel itself, though the Germans were never able to fully dominate the Channel. With Great Britain seemingly on the brink of defeat, East coast merchant convoys were particularly vulnerable to disruption and passing through the Dover–Calais narrows was temporarily abandoned. However, the coal required in the south-east remained unwavering and six days out of seven, merchant ships sailed from the Firth of Forth to the Thames estuary.

The invasion of Norway in April 1940 – which will be covered in a separate volume – taxed the major surface units of the Kriegsmarine to the fullest and nearly destroyed its destroyer flotillas, leaving the task of attacking the enemy largely to the *Schnellboote* that, after the successful invasion of The Netherlands, Belgium and France, were based in harbours stretching all the way to Brittany. With the occupation of France and the Channel Islands, regular German supply convoys also required close escort, another task allocated to the small craft of the patrol boat and submarine hunter flotillas.

Following the heavy casualties in Norway, in mid-1940 the Kriegsmarine was ordered to prepare for Operation *Sealion* and an amphibious invasion of Britain. Despite being clearly unprepared for such an enterprise, plans were hastily drawn up which would have utilized what remained of the German fleet before being, fortunately, postponed indefinitely.

A typical *U-Boot Jäger* (submarine hunter). Converted trawlers were used extensively as *Vorpostenboote* (patrol boats), *U-boot Jäger* and minesweepers, as well as the myriad craft utilized by harbour protection flotillas. Captured or commandeered vessels from occupied countries bolstered Kriegsmarine numbers considerably, yet requirements always outstripped availability. (Naval History and Heritage Command)

FLEET FIGHTING POWER

THE SHIPS

As with any story of Kriegsmarine actions, the forces involved were generally not of one single fleet, but rather an array of ships that ranged from battleships (briefly) and cruisers to the converted fishing boats of the German *Vorpostenboot* Flotillas.

Heavy Ships

The North Sea saw operations by battleships *Scharnhorst* and *Gneisenau* during 1939 and 1940 before the pair broke out into the Atlantic Ocean for distant convoy raiding. The design aspects of these battleships has already been covered more extensively in the previous book: Fleet 11: *Kriegsmarine Atlantic command, 1939–42* as has the heavy cruiser *Admiral Hipper*, which also saw brief action in the North Sea. They were not, however, truly part of the coastal battle that would develop along Britain's North Sea and Channel fringe and therefore space is not given to their design characteristics here.

Light Cruisers

Following the end of hostilities in 1918, replacement vessels for the small and largely obsolete Reichsmarine were strictly defined in Article 190 of the Treaty:

> Germany is forbidden to construct or acquire any warships other than those intended to replace the units in commission provided for in Article 181 of the present Treaty. The warships intended for replacement purposes as above shall not exceed the following displacement:
> Armoured ships 10,000 tons
> Light cruisers 6,000 tons
> Destroyers 800 tons
> Torpedo boats 200 tons

The light cruiser *Emden* photographed in China during its fourth international training/goodwill voyage. *Emden* had been the first new cruiser built by the Reichsmarine, commissioned into service on 15 October 1925. (Svintage Archive / Alamy Stock Photo)

Except where a ship has been lost, units of the different classes shall only be replaced at the end of a period of twenty years in the case of battleships and cruisers, and fifteen years in the case of destroyers and torpedo boats, counting from the launching of the ship.

Since the six light cruisers that Germany still possessed after 1918 had been launched between 1899 and 1902, they were soon eligible for replacement. The first new ship launched by the Reichsmarine was the light cruiser *Emden* in January 1925, commissioned on 15 October that year.

Germany's light cruiser force was intended to number a total of 44 ships by the end of the ambitious – and theoretical – 'Z-Plan' building drive, which would have established a balanced German fleet by 1948. This plan, however, was dependent on Hitler's 'guarantee' that there would be no war with Great Britain before 1944 at the earliest. Instead, as Britain and France declared war on Germany on 3 September 1939, the Kriegsmarine only had six light cruisers that had been commissioned between 1925 and 1935. *Emden* had been designed to conform to the strict limitations imposed by the Treaty of Versailles, sporting single gun turrets and coming in under the 6,000-ton limit, to ensure that Germany adhered to the definition of standard displacement within the Washington Treaty on the Limitation of Armament of 1922 (of which Germany was not a signatory).[2] In essence, *Emden* was created along the lines of an updated World War I design, but fulfilled its primary pre-war task of training voyages; making nine foreign cruises under various commanders that had fought the previous war and would feature heavily in the next, such as Lothar von Arnauld de la Perière – the highest scoring U-boat Ace of World War I, and therefore the most successful ever – and Karl Dönitz, who would later command the U-boat service and then the Kriegsmarine as a whole. *Emden* carried eight 15cm SK/L45 main guns that were upgraded in 1942 to the more modern 15cm TbtsK C/36 weapons, which had also been earmarked as main armament on new Type 1936A (Mob) destroyers.

---

2   The Treaty defined standard displacement as 'the displacement of the ship complete, fully manned, engined, and equipped ready for sea, including all armament and ammunition, equipment, outfit, provisions and fresh water for crew, miscellaneous stores and implements of every description that are intended to be carried in war, but <u>without</u> fuel or reserve feed water on board. The word "ton" in the present Treaty, except in the expression "metric tons", shall be understood to mean the ton of 2240 pounds (1016 kilos)'.

After *Emden*, Kriegsmarine planners created three ships of the Königsberg Class – *Königsberg*, *Karlsruhe* and *Köln* – which, though they exceeded the 6,000-ton limit, were still designed with adherence in mind. The resultant ships were compromises with three triple turrets carrying the main armament of nine 15cm SK C/25 guns, but electric welding was employed to save weight. However, miscalculations in the design process resulted in all three ships possessing inherent hull weaknesses that would severely impact on their combat utility. Like *Emden*, they were used before World War II for foreign training cruises, which soon highlighted the ships' flaws, and were also deployed as part of the somewhat cynical international non-interventionist patrols during the Spanish Civil War.

A crewman of the light cruiser *Königsberg* during its goodwill visit to Britain in July 1934; the first since the end of World War I. This *Obergefreiter* posing in front of two Grenadier Guardsmen is a qualified radio-telegraphist, he wears the National Sports Badge and also has the badge on his upper arm denoting him as command staff personnel. Major international training voyages were combined with ambassadorial visits to foreign ports by Germany's light cruisers. (Oleg Konin / Alamy Stock Photo)

The next design – Leipzig Class, of which only the namesake cruiser was built – also took part in Spanish patrols, but severe damage inflicted by heavy weather during a transit of the Bay of Biscay highlighted the continuing problem of compromised structural integrity. Only one training cruise to Tangiers in the spring of 1939 was undertaken before war broke out. After some years, scheduled remedial strengthening treatment was never carried out due to the deteriorating war situation.

The last light cruiser that was built by the Kriegsmarine was the *Nürnberg*; an improved Leipzig-class ship, generally named as belonging to its own Nürnberg class. However, though some improvements were tangible, structural weaknesses persisted, necessitating a reduced fuel load and therefore limited cruising range. *Nürnberg* was commissioned into the Kriegsmarine on 2 November 1935 and, as the newest of the light cruisers, became the flagship for Commander of Scouting Forces (*Befehlshaber der Aufklärungsstreitkräfte*); a post occupied by *Vizeadmiral* Hermann Densch at the outbreak of war, who was replaced by *Konteradmiral* Günther Lütjens in October 1939. Ultimately, the Kriegsmarine's light cruiser story is one of limited employment opportunity and, predominantly, failure.

Destroyers

Destroyers had been defined in the London Naval Treaty of 1930 as 'surface vessels of war the standard displacement of which does not exceed 1,850 tons and with a gun not above 5.1 inch (130 mm) calibre'. During much of the interwar period, the larger class of Pre-1914 torpedo boats retained by the Reichsmarine fulfilled a stop-gap purpose as de-facto destroyers. The Kriegsmarine did not begin the construction of purpose-built fleet destroyers until 1934. At that time, German military theoreticians considered the most likely enemies would be France or Poland, meaning that newly designed

A type 34 destroyer in harbour. Number 1 gun is missing from this ship. (Author's collection)

destroyers would need a radius of action of around 1,000 miles, thereby giving access to the limits of the North and Baltic Seas. They required a high speed to enable the traditional role of screening fleet battleships, such as the planned *Scharnhorst*, as well as allowing fast, offensive minelaying, which was to be the cornerstone of immediate coastal strategy.

The resultant Type 34 design presented a compromise between speed, range and offensive striking power while keeping construction time and cost to an acceptable level. Raeder had already decided to exceed Versailles limitations when he agreed to a ship displacing 1,850 tons and carrying a main armament of five 12.7cm SK C/34 guns, two quadruple 53.3cm torpedo tube installations, four 3.7cm SK C/30s in twin mountings and six individually mounted 2cm C/30 flak weapons. Four depth charge launchers on each side of the rear deckhouse were augmented by six individual racks on each stern flank, and either 32 or 64 depth charges could be carried. Stern rails allowed minelaying and 60 could be carried. The destroyer was powered by what turned out to be untried and highly temperamental high-pressure Wagner steam turbines that caused constant problems during their operational lifespan. With such heavy armament and theoretical capabilities, planners intended that the Type 34 could almost act like a miniature cruiser in a fleet setting, though its performance did not live up to expectations.

The first Type 34 – *Z1 Leberecht Maass* – was commissioned on 14 January 1937 and became the flagship for *Führer der Torpedoboote*, under whose command they operated, before beginning combined trials and training. Interestingly, German Imperial Navy tradition had not named ships below cruiser size, but the Reichsmarine ignored this tradition and the early destroyers up to Z23 were all named after officers of the Imperial Navy. Unfortunately, the ship's seakeeping qualities were below expectations; the destroyer shipped much water over the bow in high seas and was difficult to handle as it was top heavy with such extensive armament on a relatively narrow hull. A short forecastle and lack of flare at the bow exacerbated poor handling and the addition of a *staukeil* – a short keel with a wedge-shaped cross section – was added under the transom from Z5 onwards to improve the ships' turning circle by deflecting propellor wash downwards, thereby lifting the stern. In practice, however, this merely caused the bow to dig further into the sea, making the number 1 gun position unworkable as well as rendering the destroyer extremely difficult to control. Furthermore, it placed unnatural stress on the midships hull which subsequently required strengthening. After the first four Type 34s entered service in 1937, the remaining 12 that had been ordered were already having design alterations, thereafter, becoming the Type 34A, a slightly modified bow the most obvious change above the waterline. The last of this first destroyer building drive – *Z16 Friedrich Eckoldt* – was commissioned on 28 July 1938.

With destroyers now being thoroughly tested by their new crews, a fresh design was created that became the Type 36, of which six were constructed (*Z17 Diether von Roeder–Z22 Anton Schmitt*). These were improved and enlarged versions of the Type 34/34A with top weight reduced by cutting down the funnels and altering the bridge structure. They had an increased beam, more sheer on the bow (the final three being given 'clipper bows') and a slightly reworked hull shape. Despite the fact that they retained the overly complicated and troublesome steam turbine systems, the Type 36 was a marked improvement, with the larger hull providing increased fuel bunkerage and therefore greater operating range. The last of this six was commissioned on 24 September 1939, bringing Germany's destroyer strength to 22, grouped into four flotillas.

The next step in the design chain came with the Type 36A, which was, once again, a slightly modified version of the previous class. Thus far, destroyers already commissioned had proved unsuitable for potential Atlantic operations both in range and seaworthiness, and work had concentrated on a Type 37 capable of such far-reaching missions. However, the balance between speed, size, range and offensive power eluded the Kriegsmarine, and work instead began on the 36A.

Eight were commissioned by November 1941 (*Z23–Z30*, reverting to the tradition of not naming ships of this size) and they were slightly larger in anticipation of being fitted with larger main guns. Five 15cm TBK C/36 guns were intended to be installed, two in a double turret at the bow and three single turrets, but a shortage of the required double turrets meant that seven of the eight destroyers sailed with four main guns, a single open-shield gun in the bow Number 1 position (*Z23* the exception, the double turret installed during a refit in 1942). However, all Type 36A ships showed even worse handling characteristics than their predecessors due to the extra armament weight. When *Z23* sailed with its double

The Type 36 destroyer *Z21 Wilhelm Heidkamp*. Following the loss of *Z1 Leberecht Maass*, *Heidkamp* became the flagship of *Führer der Torpedoboote Konteradmiral* Günther Lütjens. In a break from Imperial Naval tradition, the first 21 destroyers of the Kriegsmarine received a name as well as number. This vessel was named after *Obermaschinist* Wilhelm Heidkamp who had saved his ship *SMS Seydlitz* from exploding by flooding the magazines despite the valve he turned glowing red hot. Despite his hands and lungs being severely injured, he survived the war but died in 1931 from the lung disease that was a legacy of his actions. (Author's collection)

turret, the ship's performance reached a critically bad level, and the installation of further double turrets was abandoned. Continuing design alterations resulted in the Type 36A (Mob) model, but only two were commissioned by the end of 1942 and neither saw action outside of the Baltic until 1943.

Unlike some flotilla organizations that fluctuated in size due to being purely logistical groupings (such as U-boats), an early war destroyer flotilla had an intended strength of six ships. This was accomplished by combining two divisions of three each. For example, the 1st Destroyer Flotilla was formed in 1938 by the combination of 1st Destroyer and 3rd Destroyer Divisions. Flotillas could and did act as cohesive units, but were also formed into ad-hoc battlegroups dependent on ship serviceability and availability at the time of any given operation.

Torpedo Boats

During World War I, Germany fielded 244 destroyers and torpedo boats. Of these, only 32 torpedo boats – built before 1914 – were retained by the Reichsmarine under Versailles Treaty terms, which had limited German destroyers to 800 tons and torpedo boats to 200. The allowable strength was not to exceed a total of 12 destroyers and 12 torpedo boats in commission at any one time, with a further four of each type in reserve.

In essence, torpedo boats were mini-destroyers, a concept largely abandoned by most other navies. Nonetheless, Germany still considered them to be a viable class of warship. Intended to be capable of fleet operations, they were also meant to display fast, defensive coastal capabilities, their primary torpedo weaponry posing a great potential threat to any enemy capital ships that should venture into German sea areas.

By the mid-1920s, replacement of the aged torpedo boats retained by the Reichsmarine had become imperative and six Type 23 *Raubvogel* (Bird of Prey) class torpedo boats began construction; *Möwe* (Gull) was the first to be launched on 24 March 1926. Built with a flush-deck hull, they were just over

Commissioned in 1929, *Leopard* here flies the flag of the Reichsmarine. One of the second design models – the Type 24 *Raubtier* class – *Leopard* had taken part in patrols during the Spanish Civil War and was extensively involved in stop and search missions in the Skagerrak during 1939. *Leopard* was sunk on 30 April 1940 when it was accidentally rammed by minelayer *Preussen* following a minelaying mission in the Skagerrak. Difficult to handle at the best of times, the torpedo boat's rudder failed and the ship ran into *Preussen*'s bow. A single officer was killed in the accident: *Leutnant zur See* Gernot Marschall, oldest son of Fleet Commander *Vizeadmiral* Wilhelm Marschall. (Getty Images)

87m in length with a beam of 8.25m. The Type 23 series displaced between 798 and 924 tons, carrying three 10.5cm SK L/45 main guns (one forward and two aft), two banks of triple 53.3cm torpedo tubes and capacity for 30 mines. A pair of 2cm flak weapons was added in 1931, and further firepower modifications were made after war broke out in 1939. Powered by two shaft-geared turbines, the torpedo boat could muster 24kts at full speed, but suffered from difficult handling characteristics, reportedly almost impossible to hold on course in strong wind or at low speed.

Repeating the pattern of destroyer development, while these first six were under construction an improved Type 24 *Raubtier* (Carnivore) class was in design; slightly larger and carrying the new 10.5cm SK C/28 main armament, though ammunition shortages would prove problematic as the weapon was never in widespread usage. Six of this model were also built, the first – *Iltis* (Polecat) – was commissioned on 1 October 1928.

After the last of this latter class entered service, all 12 vessels were grouped into the 2nd, 3rd and 4th Torpedo Boat flotillas and future torpedo boat constructive capability was instead diverted to 'proper' destroyers and S-boats. Larger destroyers were considered more suitable to counter likely French and Polish equivalent vessels, while S-boats were cheaper to produce, required fewer crew and were extremely capable of coastal torpedo warfare. The sole area in which S-boats were considered inappropriate was the central North Sea which could at times experience extremely harsh weather.

On 22 April 1935, the German government bluntly informed Britain that it intended to construct 12 destroyers and two cruisers. British foreign policy was undecided over whether to maintain the hard line established at Versailles or instead opt for appeasement and attempt to tame a resurgent Germany. This indecision was no doubt compounded by a subsequent announcement that 12 U-boats would also be built – for which the components had already been constructed: a clear violation of the Treaty of Versailles. The resulting negotiations between Berlin and London yielded the Anglo-German Naval Agreement signed on 18 June 1935, which accepted a rebuilt German Navy, limited to a total tonnage equivalent to 35 per cent of

Schnellboot S8 in the North Sea. Launched in 1934, S8 was the second of the 1933 S7 Class; the first S-boats to be equipped with marine diesels. Lengthened from its predecessors to 32.4m overall and the beam increased to 4.9m, it displaced 59 tons and was crewed by 21 men. The three lightweight MAN L7 Zn 19/30 two-stroke diesel engines ultimately proved inadequate, reaching only 32kts. A 'knuckle' had been introduced into the bow to increase seaworthiness and prevent the bow from 'burying' into heavy waves; a problem that had presented itself in trials of previous models. (M&N / Alamy Stock Photo)

the Royal Navy. This tonnage limitation applied to each type of vessel; cruisers and destroyers combined into the same category.[3] In May 1935 Adolf Hitler publicly announced the rearmament of Germany and the abrogation of the Treaty of Versailles; the Reichsmarine was officially renamed the Kriegsmarine and governmental funding for its reconstruction was increased.

Using the refreshed tonnage limitations and extra monetary source, torpedo boats were reconsidered. Capable of being built relatively cheaply in large numbers, they could handle both convoy escort duty and offensive torpedo missions at a range greater than that of S-boats. By freeing fleet destroyers from those duties, combined with a complicated restructuring of the Kriegsmarine tonnage allowance listed in the Anglo-German Naval Agreement, the result was resumption of torpedo boat construction. The first of the newly designed Type 35 – T1 – was laid down in Elbing on 14 November 1936, though it was not launched until after war was declared. Twelve of this class were completed and another nine of the slightly improved Type 37, which began commissioning in 1941.

These two types both carried reduced main armament, with a single stern-mounted 10.5cm SK C/32, as any forward guns were considered likely to make the low-freeboard flush-deck design unstable. Anti-aircraft defence comprised a single 3.7cm SK C/30 on the aft deckhouse and two 2cm C/30 guns in the bridge wings. Offensive emphasis lay on its torpedo armament, which still comprised two banks of three tubes mounted midships, and a potential load of 30 mines. Like all torpedo boats, no consideration was given at any point to ASW (anti-submarine warfare) defence, and between 1935 and 1941 none were equipped with depth charges.

However, combat experience showed that these ships, despite having improved sea-keeping qualities over predecessors, were largely a wasted effort for the Kriegsmarine's limited construction and crewing capacities. S-boats proved more seaworthy than expected, and the torpedo boats too slow and unwieldy for the kind of high-speed coastal warfare for which they had been predominantly intended. In hindsight, the resources expended on creating and maintaining these ships could have better been used elsewhere. Yet, they were not the biggest design disappointment. That distinction would be saved for the Fleet Escort.

Fleet Escort

The *Flottenbegleiter* (Fleet Escort) had been developed for Naval Security Forces during the early 1930s; purpose-built fleet escorts the principal role of which was to provide a fast inner screen for *Panzerschiffe* (*Deutschland*, *Admiral Scheer* and *Admiral Graf Spee*) while also being capable of minesweeping and ASW work. A design limit on this new class was a displacement not exceeding 600 tons,

---

[3] U-boats were also thus constrained, though there was a clause by which Germany could possess a tonnage equal to Great Britain under undefined 'extraordinary circumstances'.

as ships of that size were unregulated by the London Treaty of 1930 that sought to limit international shipbuilding. The concept was sound, as later evidenced by Allied frigate and destroyer-escort types; however, the German effort was a complete failure.

Planning was completed by 1934 and ten ships ordered; the first, F1, was launched on 1 March 1935 and commissioned the following December. By the middle of August 1938, the final ship (F10) had been commissioned, though the entire class had already been found to be unreliable and not fit for purpose. Although 17 were originally planned, their exceedingly poor performance led to cancellation of all further construction. Like Germany's destroyers, they were top heavy and too slow and cumbersome for their planned role. The keel system hampered seaworthiness, causing the ships to bury their noses in all but calm seas. They were, therefore, too unstable to provide effective anti-aircraft defence or allow for successful minelaying. Their minesweeping capabilities were, at best, mediocre and they lacked the necessary detection equipment to become effective ASW vessels.

They carried two 10.5cm SK L/45 C/32 cannon in shielded single mounts, four 3.7cm Flak SK L/83 C/30s in twin mounts and four 2cm single flak weapons, and had capacity for up to 62 mines. The installation of stern mine rails caused the aft 10.5cm gun to be mounted a deck higher than originally planned. Plans to include torpedo tubes were scrapped as it would have pushed the ship over its official 600-ton displacement, which it had already unofficially exceeded. The *Flottenbegleiter* were 75.94m overall, capable of a top speed of 28kts and manned by a crew of 121 men. They had no bilge keels, but instead a new type of Frahm anti-roll system was fitted, which would prove a costly failure as it was overly complex and decreased stability with the slightest handling error. The *Flottenbegleiter* were also used as test beds for newly designed high-pressure steam power plants, but they too had proved highly temperamental and were prone to frequent breakdowns, so much so that sailors disparagingly referred to the unlucky units as 'Horst Wessel flotilla', because they marched with the fleet 'only in spirit'.

The existing *Flottenbegleiter* were swiftly delegated to various non-combatant roles until forced back to the front line to bolster an already under-equipped Kriegsmarine in September 1939. Grouped into a single *Geleitflottille*, it served within the North Sea under *Fregattenkapitän* Friedrich-Wilhelm Pindter until his death on 14 December 1939. His successor was *Kapitänleutnant* Hagen Küster who assumed command in January 1940. Even though the ships had proved a complete failure, the idea of fleet escort ships remained alive and later several *Geleitflottille* were formed using superior captured destroyers and torpedo boats.

Flottenbegleiter F6. Only ten of this disastrous design failure were built. One was lost in action and the remainder relegated to non-combatant duties. By March 1940, the flotilla had been disbanded after their brief service in the North Sea had highlighted the ships' failings. The concept of a fast escort vessel capable of minesweeping and anti-submarine work was not entirely abandoned though, and new flotillas were created in and around the Mediterranean Sea in later years, using captured and converted vessels. (Author's collection)

Minesweepers

Even though the German military had been decimated by the Versailles Treaty, a small German minesweeping administration had been required by Article 193 to continue its work on remnants of wartime fields. Thirty-six Type 1915 and 1916 minesweepers were retained by the Reichsmarine in the 1920s as 1. M-Flotilla. Though largely used as tenders and training ships after newer minesweepers began entering service, these older ships would later return to active service with the Kriegsmarine to bolster fleet numbers.

New minesweepers were an integral part of Germany's ambitious naval-building drive and the M35 class was developed along similar lines as proven World War I vessels. These ships had a full load displacement of over 870 tons, carried heavy armaments for a minesweeper with two 10.5cm cannon, one 3.7cm and two 2cm flak weapons, enabling them to tangle with enemy destroyers. A multi-purpose design, they could be fitted for minelaying and were able to carry 30 mines on hull rails as well as four depth charge launchers for ASW work. The hull itself was of steel construction, divided into 12 watertight compartments, while a double bottom covered most of the ships' waterline length. The first nine minesweepers of this class were ordered on 22 November 1935, and in total, 69 were commissioned between 1938 and 1943. M1 was launched in Hamburg on 5 March 1937 and completed by September 1938.

The M35 class was constructed in three different series: Type 1935, ordered between 1935 and 1936; Type 1938 with increased hull dimensions providing better seakeeping qualities and allowing for the installation of additional generators for magnetic sweeps; and Type 1939 (Mob), which had been ordered after the outbreak of war with emphasis on simplified construction. All were powered by Vertical Triple Expansion (VTE) Engines and oil-burning boilers that required skilled maintenance and operation, capable of reaching 18kts.

However, while large minesweepers were ideal within the North Sea, a new class of smaller vessels with a weak magnetic signature was needed for shallow coastal waters, resulting in the *Räumboot*. Of similar appearance and design lineage to a motor torpedo boat, the prototype R1 was commissioned during 1931. The craft had a composite hull of double-skinned wood on light metal framing, the hull 24.5m overall length, with a beam of 4.38m and a draught of 1.22m under deep load. Armed with a single 20mm cannon (upgraded to two from R17 onwards and then progressively up-gunned

M35 class minesweepers of the 2nd Minesweeping Flotilla, led by M6 at the front. The first new minesweepers built by the Kriegsmarine, the M35 type proved to be a robust and versatile ship, capable of its intended minesweeping task, as well as minelaying, convoy escort and submarine hunting. M6 was lost after hitting a mine off Lorient, France, on 23 October 1941. (Hutton Archive)

during the war) and crewed by 15 to 18 men, R1 reached a maximum of 17kts with her 700hp MWM diesels and could deploy sweeping gear in a sea state up to 6 on the Beaufort Scale. It was an extremely effective vessel.

Sea experience led to specifications progressively altering; R16 measured 27.8m long, had the same beam as originally designed but had an increased draught of 1.36m under full load and a displacement of 52.5 tons. An early model, R8, was of slightly wider beam and had also been fitted with Voith Schneider propellers that delivered thrust in all directions and combined propulsion and steering into a single unit. Vessels so equipped did not require rudders; propeller blades protruded at right angles from a rotor casing and rotated around a vertical axis. The superb manoeuvrability that these provided proved highly successful and they were installed from R17 onwards on most boats. However, with material shortages towards the end of the war, those constructed from 1944 reverted to conventional twin-shaft screws.

Räumboote, like S-boats, operated in pairs – a *Rotte* – and as well as sweeping, were used for minelaying (capable of carrying 12 mines), ASW patrols and convoy escort. Eight depth charges could be accommodated, launched by simply being rolled overboard.

Converted trawlers of different specifications were also commonly used by the Kriegsmarine as minesweepers, as well as for other Security Division components such as *Vorpostenboote* (patrol boats) and *U-Boot Jäger* (submarine hunters). Their configuration could be so similar that it was often difficult to distinguish one class of vessel from another. With a desire for German self-sufficiency, the Nazis had actively encouraged an expansion of Germany's deep-sea fishing fleet in the late 1930s; trawlers of 400 GRT displacement becoming a standard design and later frequently commandeered for miliary use. With the occupation of western Europe, suitable vessels for requisitioning as minesweepers were

R41 ENGAGES THE ENEMY NEAR BARFLEUR, 19 JUNE 1942 (overleaf)

As part of their multi-purpose capability, *Räumboote* were frequently used as convoy escort. On 19 June 1942, the freighter MV *Turquoise* – an 810 GRT Belgian ship that had been scuttled at the time of the German invasion and subsequently repaired by the Kriegsmarine – was travelling to the Channel Islands with supplies for the German garrison. *Räumboote* of Boulogne's 4th *Räumboote* Flotilla and auxiliary minesweepers of 38th Minesweeping Flotilla based in Le Havre acted as escorts.

That night they were intercepted by a Royal Navy group on an offensive Channel patrol east of Barfleur in the Seine Bay. Hunt-class destroyer HMS *Albrighton* and two accompanying steam gunboats – SG7 and SG8 – attacked the convoy during the early morning. In the battle that followed, R41 and MV *Turquoise* were hit and sunk by torpedoes, minesweeper M3800 (an ex-Dutch pilot vessel) was damaged and MV *Turquoise* damaged and beached near St Vlaast to prevent sinking. The British lost SG7, commanded by Sub-Lieutenant R. Barnet, RNVR, which was severely damaged by gunfire and scuttled with 27 men taken prisoner.

Räumboote in action. These versatile minesweepers were used in every European, Scandinavian and North African theatre of action in which the Kriegsmarine fought. (DPE Picture Alliance / Alamy Stock Photo)

hurriedly inspected. For traditional trawler forms, conversion work was relatively standardized; the deckhouse was converted for use as a radio-room, complete with hydrophone receiver if available, while a ridged wheelhouse was added above. This allowed unobstructed vision over the forward gun platform that carried the boat's main deck armament. The wheelhouse would in turn be crowned with a signal mast. The stern was structurally altered to accommodate minesweeping equipment, while *Schleppspulgerät* (SSG), towed magnetic loop gear, was housed in the deckhouse. Like larger minesweepers, trawlers were equipped with MES (*Minen Eigenschutze Anlage*) degaussing gear that reduced the ship's magnetic signature.

Generally, auxiliary minesweepers had insubstantial armament; a 37mm flak cannon mounted on the forecastle, 20mm flak cannon abaft of this and a further 20mm flak cannon behind the wheelhouse. This, however, varied depending on what was available locally. Some were issued with larger calibre 88mm or 105mm cannon, which were often captured models as there were frequent shortages of weapon supplies. Two depth charge throwers with three projectiles each were astern to port and starboard, while the holds were converted for ammunition storage and accommodation for about 25 men.

This requisitioning drive placed certain strains on both the local economy and that of the Third Reich. Military vessels could be seized as legitimate spoils of war, whereas vessels requisitioned from private individuals or companies required financial compensation. For example, the Dutch tugboat *Cycloop* belonging to the salvage firm Doeksen & Zoon was requisitioned by the Kriegsmarine on 4 September 1940 and numbered *R46S* for use as a gunnery target tow. The cost of the requisition was Hfl 28.05 per day; a payment maintained until the end of the war. Coupled with this financial burden was the effect on local food supplies and trade as merchant and fishing vessels were removed for military service.

Schnellboote

The same design tree that had led to the *Räumboote* gave birth to the *Schnellboote* – an offensive motor torpedo boat, known to the Allies as an E-boat. Pre-war design work had been facilitated by this class of vessel – a 'torpedo boat' not exceeding 200 tons displacement – not explicitly covered by the terms of the Versailles Treaty. Germany had used small motorboats during World War I and in the postwar Reichsmarine immediately began experimenting with fresh speedboat concepts, taking strong cues from the British and Italian navies.

Following several design applications of a small craft with a planing hull and with knowledge that future German MTBs were most likely to operate within the North Sea which frequently was beset by heavy swells, the Lürssen company's displacement hull was chosen by the Reichsmarine as the starting point for S-boat design. Constructed of wooden planking over alloy frames, the boat was lightweight, increasing its overall speed and performance and capable of bearing the weight of two forward-firing torpedo tubes mounted towards the bow. On 7 August 1930, the boat named UZ(S)16 was commissioned into the Reichsmarine. On 16 March 1932, it was renamed *Schnellboot* S1.

Constructed of mahogany and light metal composite, S1 was powered by three 900hp Daimler-Benz petrol engines; both MAN and Daimler-Benz were commissioned to develop lightweight high-speed diesels, though they were not ready by the time S1 was outfitted, the first diesels were fitted from S6 onward. At 26.5m long with a beam of 4.2m and a draught of 1.1m, S1 was the largest high-speed coastal motorboat of the time, and still capable of 39.8kts. As well as two World War I vintage 50cm (19.7in) torpedo tubes – replaced by standardized 53.3cm torpedo tubes in 1933 – there was a single 2cm flak weapon on the stern deck. Crewed by 12 men, the boat was capable of operating in a sea state up to 5 on the Beaufort Scale (equating to a wind speed of between 17 and 21kts and waves up to 6ft high).

Loading a depth charge aboard a *Schnellboot*. This type of vessel was not ideally suited to submarine hunting and depth charges were sometimes fitted with floats and a timer, and dropped to deter surface pursuit. (Author's collection)

Although possessing excellent seakeeping qualities and built to a high specification, work began on an improved class almost as soon as testing had got underway on S1. During 1931, construction of the S2 Class (four boats numbered S2 to S5) started; it was commissioned into service between April and July 1932. The boat's length had been increased to 27.9m and the displacement also increased to 49 tons from 39 tons. All three main engines received superchargers and two extra rudders were added outboard on each side of the main rudder. These two smaller independent rudders were directly behind the screws and when operated at high speed they could be inclined up to 30°, keeping them horizontal in the water, creating extra water flow around the screws and diminishing the stern wake – a distinct advantage for combat craft attempting to minimize the chance of detection. Ingenious, this became known as the 'Lürssen effect'. Also, the scooped end to each torpedo tube that had featured on S1 was replaced with a vertical aperture sealed with a hinged door.

The complement aboard the new boats had increased to around 21 men and the armament changed beginning with S6; the 50cm torpedo tubes were replaced with what became the German naval standard 53.3cm (21in) tubes as well as the addition of a forward-mounted machine gun at the bow for both anti-aircraft and surface firing purposes. *Schnellboote* evolved as the war progressed, but they remained one of the most potent coastal weapons the Kriegsmarine possessed.

TECHNICAL FACTORS
Luftwaffe cooperation

At the outbreak of war, *Marinegruppenkommando West*, which was responsible for North Sea naval operations, exercised at least tacit control over several Luftwaffe maritime units. This was part of an increasingly contentious issue fought between the Kriegsmarine and the Luftwaffe which was eventually lost due to Hermann Göring's undeniable influence over Hitler's decision making.

Initially, two distinct Luftwaffe commands were established to allow smoother control over maritime air operations in the North or the Baltic Sea. These were *Führer der See-Luftstreitkräfte West* and *Führer der See-Luftstreitkräfte Ost* respectively, each tactically subordinate to the relevant regional *Marinegruppenkommando*. At the formation of the two posts *Generalmajor* Joachim Coeler was named *F.d.Luft. West*, while *Generalmajor* Hermann Bruch headed that in the east, both men having been former naval officers before transferring to the Luftwaffe. The squadrons initially under *F.d.Luft. West* included Dornier reconnaissance flying boats as well as floatplane fighters and the torpedo aircraft of *Küstenfliegergruppen* 106, 306 and 406. Most crews carried a Kriegsmarine officer as navigator/observer, providing immediate trained nautical navigation capability.

Additionally, MGK West theoretically controlled shipborne catapult aircraft belonging to *Bordfliegergruppe* 196 (Wilhelmshaven) and the two squadrons earmarked for future carrier deployment (*Trägergeschwader*) aboard the unfinished *Graf Zeppelin*: 4./186 (Junkers Ju 87) and 6./186 (Bf 109), though both spent only a very brief tenure under Kriegsmarine control before being transferred to Luftwaffe command. Outside of direct Kriegsmarine tactical control, *Luftflotte* 2 had been tasked with maritime operations, a specific subcommand – initially 10. *Fliegerdivision* but soon changed to X *Fliegerkorps* – using high-performance land-based aircraft.

Führer der See-Luftstreitkräfte West was responsible for reporting enemy merchant and naval activity in the North Sea, and in the first days of war, a picture quickly formed of considerable merchant shipping sailing in defiance of the declared blockade of Britain. The crews of *Luftflotte* 2's land-based bombers initially lacked the required naval training to guide German destroyers effectively towards suspicious merchant vessels, so the onus fell to *F.d.Luft. West*, with its contingent of Kriegsmarine observers.

Early war naval aviation units – *Küstenflieger* – combined Luftwaffe airmen with Kriegsmarine observers. Here *Oberleutnant* Wilhelm Gaul stands with his Luftwaffe squadron mates from *Küstenfliegergruppe* 106. He had served aboard torpedo boats before being transferred to the *Küstenflieger*. In late 1940, as part of Göring's drive for control over *all* aerial units, he was transferred to the Luftwaffe. (Tim Oliver / Alamy Stock Photo)

Cooperation between *Admiral* Alfred Saalwächter at MGK West and both

F.d.Luft West and *Luftflotte* 2 was initially very positive. Even though the Luftwaffe and Kriegsmarine had failed to coordinate the most basic tenets of cohesive maritime war (each used different map grids, there was no established mutual communications net, no common code or cypher system and inadequate telecommunications between operational headquarters and command stations), an element of goodwill had been fostered, not least of all due to Coeler's obvious enthusiasm for maritime operations. Overcoming difficulties imposed by joint control of naval air units, local organizational measures between the various headquarters facilitated effective cooperation. Luftwaffe and naval offices immediately exchanged grid-square charts, enabling a composite overlay to be created to ease operational coordination. Communications systems were rapidly improved upon, and a Luftwaffe liaison officer – *Oberst* Hans Metzner – was assigned to Saalwächter's staff.

During the war's early months, Luftwaffe maritime aircraft contributed greatly to the assault on Britain's east coast convoy routes, as well as periodically attacking the British fishing fleet as part of the attempt to starve Britain into submission. Aerial minelaying allowed the sowing of minefields in particularly shallow waters, although this would ultimately work against the Germans.

While torpedo and bombing missions harvested a grim tally of merchant ships, they achieved far less against Royal Navy targets. In mid-1940, British fighter defences were withdrawn inland for the Battle of Britain and Luftwaffe coastal maritime missions reached a level that was never to be repeated. Ironically, the same demand for German aircraft over southern England resulted in the decline of North Sea operations as aircraft were syphoned away from maritime units. During September 1940, Hitler attempted to quieten the fractious relationship that had developed between Raeder and Göring. In a directive issued on 13 September, Hitler recognized that, though all aerial forces needed to be consolidated under Göring's command for the concentrated attacks on Britain, the Kriegsmarine required its own reconnaissance forces under direct naval tactical command. However, with minimal naval operations possible following the battle for Norway, the *Führer* reasoned that it was therefore logical to presume that such supporting aerial reconnaissance units would probably be under-utilized, and therefore must alternate between Luftwaffe and Kriegsmarine command. Furthermore, Hitler reserved the right to decide such matters of allocation between the two service branches himself, as supreme military commander. Göring, one of the most politically adept of Wehrmacht officers, was always able to ingratiate himself with his *Führer* and maritime Luftwaffe operations steadily faded from

Signalling from an auxiliary minesweeper to a circling Junkers Ju 88. Coordination between the Luftwaffe and Kriegsmarine was frequently poor; the most extreme result of which ended with two destroyers sunk in error during 1940. (National Digital Archive, Poland)

Kriegsmarine control. Furthermore, many crews recently trained in nautical navigation and combat were wasted; lost in the subsequent futile bombing of British cities and industrial areas.

Torpedoes

Despite the first few S-boats being initially equipped in the early 1930s with surplus World War I 50cm torpedo tubes, from 1933 onwards all Kriegsmarine surface vessels used 53.3cm G7a steam-powered torpedoes, known as the 'Ato'. The electric version – G7e – could not be used because the height from which they were fired could potentially damage the batteries as it hit the sea surface.

Theoretically, the G7a was a superb weapon. Capable of 40kts, it outstripped the G7e torpedo by 10kts, though it lacked the 'wakeless' advantage of an electric motor. The G7a's turbine engine was powered by steam created by the burning of dechaydronaphthalene (alcohol) fuel mixed with compressed air. This speed was essential for a torpedo that was not only noisy but left a visible bubble track. It was capable of being gyro-angled while still in its tube to run up to 90° of its centreline, adjustable in 1° increments. Likewise, its depth settings could be adjusted in 1m steps to a theoretical maximum of 52m.

The G7a could be fitted with either an impact fuse (*Aufschlagzündung*, or AZ) or magnetic fuse (*Magnetzündung*, or MZ). The latter relied on the ship's magnetic field detonating the torpedo as it ran beneath its keel; supposedly more destructive as the explosive shock wave was amplified through water. However, an extremely lax trials regimen within the *Torpedoversuchsanstalt* (Torpedo Test Institute, TVA) meant that the weapon was inadequately tested before being put into full production, subsequently causing a crisis within the Kriegsmarine.

After mass torpedo failures, fresh tests showed the magnetic fuse to be faulty, particularly in northern latitudes. During 1936, the TVA conducted test-firings against suspended nets that showed a tendency for both G7a and G7e torpedoes to run up to 2m too deep, potentially passing under the target and failing to explode if using contact fuses. This was, incredibly, deemed acceptable by the TVA, as it would be solved by using the magnetic fuse; the same magnetic fuse that proved faulty. The issue of deep-running torpedoes would not be solved until 1942 when a U-boat crew discovered a design flaw that leaked air into the balance chamber housing a hydrostatic valve that controlled depth settings.

A destroyer launched torpedo. All Kriegsmarine surface craft used the G7a steam-propelled torpedo. Severe shortcomings in pre-war testing led to major problems in depth control and fuse reliability. (Author's collection)

To compound the problem, a new and 'improved' four-fingered AZ contact pistol was an unnecessarily complicated inter-war design completely reliant on correct depth keeping. This new pistol had replaced the reliable two-fingered version used during World War I, but it had been test fired only twice in 1937. The safety device that prevented a torpedo arming near the firing vessel was also found to be faulty. This comprised a small four-bladed propeller at the warhead's tip, spun by water movement which brought two detonator contacts together when a set number of revolutions had occurred. Theoretically, this put the torpedo 300m from its launch tube before it armed. This small propeller also then acted as the 'fingers' of the contact pistol, pushed back by impacting a solid object and firing the explosive charge. However, the propeller blades were of significantly smaller diameter than the torpedo itself. A hit on a flat target, such as Baltic target ships or deep draught vessels, would result in detonation, but striking a curved hull could result in the blades not touching the target, the torpedo then sliding underneath to pass beyond the target ship. Also, the AZ fuse was discovered to contain a fault that allowed the premature release of the firing pin, resulting in several premature detonations and potentially endangering the firing vessel while almost certainly betraying its position.

Even German aerial torpedoes were deeply flawed. Latecomers in the field of torpedo aircraft, the Luftwaffe maritime units used a 45cm aerial torpedo designated LT (*Luft Torpedo*) F5. However, this 650kg weapon had limited drop-parameters that required a drop speed not exceeding 75kts (140km/h) and a height of between 15 and 20m from sea level. A minimum water depth of more than 23m was required for the torpedo's initial drop, which negated all effectiveness in shallow coastal waters such as found on Britain's North Sea coast. A marked lack of cooperation between the Kriegsmarine and Luftwaffe frustrated testing and it was spectacularly unsuccessful when first used. The Luftwaffe failed to appreciate the true value of the aerial torpedo, believing that the same results were achievable using less-costly bombs.

During March the LT F5 was upgraded (to LT F5a), which included major alterations to the rudder, though its performance remained substandard. Interservice bickering and a lack of cooperation between the Kriegsmarine and Luftwaffe resulted in an absence of technical development of this weapon, though the Luftwaffe had also shown little interest in carrying out the required research work before 1941. When they finally did so, Kriegsmarine testing data already accrued by naval establishments was withheld from the Luftwaffe's Technical Division. With such a disastrous torpedo situation, it is no surprise that mines were the most effective weapon in the German arsenal during 1939 and 1940.

Loading EMC mines aboard an S-boat in a French harbour. (Author's collection)

Mines

Minesweeping had been the one branch of the Reichsmarine that remained functioning at a high level following the end of World War I. Correspondingly, research into the destruction – and creation – of various mine types had been

BRITISH EAST COAST CONVOY ROUTE AND GERMAN DESTROYER MINEFIELDS

continued without pause since the end of hostilities. Highly efficient contact mines had already been in use during World War I, but Allied minesweeping limited their effectiveness and therefore the development of influence triggers became a German priority.

The physical damage caused by naval mines can be divided into three categories. The first is that of a contact mine which simply blasts a hole in a ship's hull, injuring crewmen with the blast itself and accompanying shrapnel and possibly sinking the target vessel. The second is the pressure wave from an influence mine exploding a short distance from its target. The primary explosive pressure wave travels at the speed of sound in all directions, an incandescent steam bubble forming at the point of detonation which then quickly collapses due to the water pressure differential, creating a water column. If this occurs beneath the centre of a ship, it will lift the ship centre upwards, weakening the keel, and as the bubble collapses the ship centre will fall into the void, breaking the keel and splitting the ship in half. The bubble can also attach to a ship's hull, like the result of a depth charge near miss, which upon collapsing forms a high-energy jet of water that can punch a hole straight through the hull, instantly killing any person in its path. The third is a shock wave of a mine exploding some distance from a ship's hull that can cause the entire ship to resonate, shaking everything onboard to such an extent that machinery can be disabled and hull plates fractured.

Kriegsmarine surface forces within the North Sea and English Channel utilized several different mine types. The EM series of mines (*Elektrische Minen*) comprised 13 different types of moored contact mines (except the EMS series, which were drifting contact mines not used until 1943), capable of being laid by both surface craft and U-boats. The buoyant spherical mine body was attached by cable to a cradle that would break free when dropped in the water, anchoring on the seabed and allowing the mine to rise to whatever required depth the cable allowed. Contact mines used a chemical horn to detonate the charge; a hollow lead finger containing a glass vial filled with sulphuric acid. When the horn is broken the vial breaks allowing the acid to run down a tube into a lead-acid battery that contained no acid electrolyte. The sulphuric acid energizes the battery, detonating the explosive. The EMA mine was armed when the anchor and mine casing separated, drawing a safety pin from the arming switch and completing the circuit from the horn batteries to the detonator.

The EMC mine had three separate variations: 'EMC m KA' that incorporated a 30m tube over the upper portion of the mooring wire that closed a circuit and exploded the mine if encountering a sweep; 'EMC m *Kette*' (chain) that

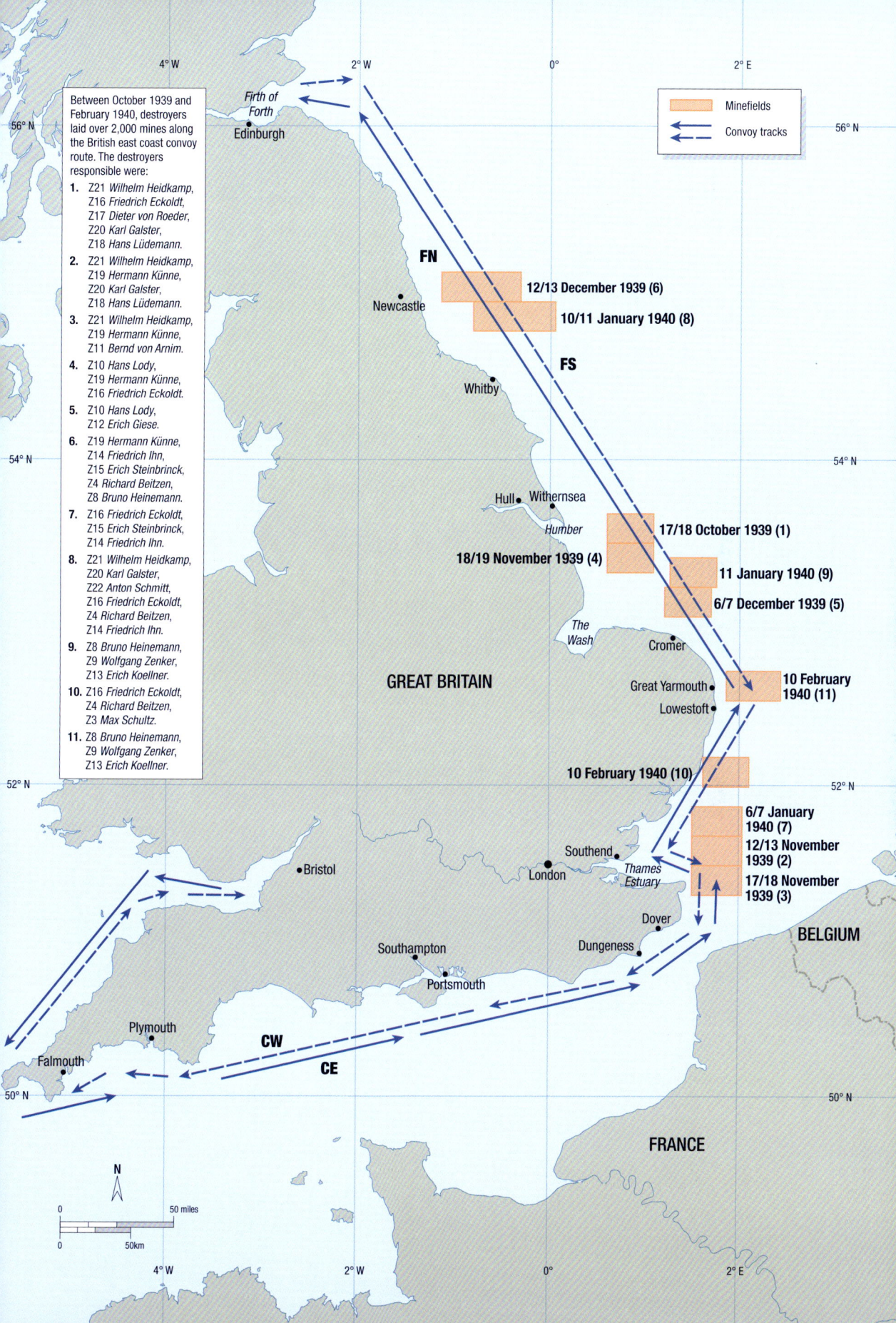

incorporated an upper portion of 6m of chain to make sweeping more difficult; and 'EMC m AN Z' that could be moored in up to 350m of water and was activated not by horns, but by upper and lower antennae.

The first influence mine in use was the EMF, an oblong mine 114cm in diameter, 127cm long. The mine became active when mooring tension pulled out a spindle, tripping a lever that released locking balls from an internal clockwork spindle. Water pressure depressed the clock spindle at a depth of 5m, starting the clock which counted down a delay period allowing the laying vessel to clear the area. Once that period had expired, the unit began a testing cycle. If it failed to orient itself properly after a pre-set time of up to 12 hours, a scuttling charge fired to sink the mine.

The spherical UM series of anti-submarine mines (*U-boots wehrmine*) could be laid at variable depths depending on the amount of mooring cable. The hemispheric RM influence ground mine series included the RMA – known as the *Schildköte* (turtle mine) – the slightly smaller RMB and wood-cased RMH designed to both reduce detection by minesweeper and cater for a potential shortage of metal. Using magnetic fuses, these mines were also capable of being controlled and fired by observers via cable. Ground mines were for use when water depth did not exceed 60m or so.

The LM series were parachute mines – *Luft Minen* – to be dropped by the Luftwaffe. However, the relatively small LMA magnetic influence mine was sometimes modified for delivery by S-boat; redesignated 'LMA/S'.

EMC mines loaded aboard a torpedo boat of the 2nd T-Flotilla. (Author's collection)

GERMAN DESIGNATION	TYPE	TRIGGER	EXPLOSIVE CHARGE (HEXANITE)
EMA	Moored mine	Contact (5 chemical horns)	150kg
EMB	Moored mine	Contact (7 chemical horns)	220kg
EMC	Moored mine	Contact (8 chemical horns)	300kg
EMD	Moored mine	Contact (5 chemical horns)	150kg
EMF	Moored mine	Magnetic	340kg
LMA	Aerial (parachute), ground mine	Magnetic	300kg
LMA/S	Aerial, modified for surface laying, ground mine	Magnetic	300kg
UMA	Moored anti-submarine mine	Contact (8 horns – 5 chemical, 3 switch)	30kg
UMA (K)	Moored mine	Contact (6 horns – 5 chemical, 1 switch)	40kg

GERMAN DESIGNATION	TYPE	TRIGGER	EXPLOSIVE CHARGE (HEXANITE)
UMB	Moored mine	Contact (8 horns – 5 chemical, 3 switch)	40kg
RMA	Ground mine	Magnetic (also able to be fired by observation)	795kg
RMB	Ground mine	Magnetic (also able to be fired by observation)	455kg
RMH	Ground mine	Magnetic (also able to be fired by observation)	900kg

Unfortunately for the efficiency of the German minelaying offensive, a major weakness in its implementation was the lack of a centralized Mining Command. Though OKM's Mine Department – *Amtsgruppe Sperrwaffen*, headed by *Konteradmiral* Fritz Lamprecht – held control over the materials for mine construction, operationally there was little cohesion between the Kriegsmarine and Luftwaffe. No specially built, high-speed minelaying vessels had been constructed. Instead, naval minelaying was handled by light cruisers, U-boats, converted merchantmen, destroyers, torpedo boats, S-boats and minesweepers down to R-boat size. None was ever available in sufficient numbers to meet requirements, nor, for that matter, were mines. Furthermore, with obvious immediate goals in mind, mines designed to sink merchant shipping were prioritized over those that could have disabled British minesweepers and potentially aided a concerted mining offensive.

The Luftwaffe insisted on independence in minelaying, though aircraft of X *Fliegerkorps* earmarked for the task displayed an excellent level of initial cooperation with SKL and, despite wishing to stockpile a large number of mines before sowing, bowed to naval pressure and began aerial mining in November 1939. On 20 November, four biplane Heinkel He 59s laid mines in the Thames estuary; further missions were flown on the nights of 22 and 23 November. Between 20 November and 7 December five missions were flown in which 46 LMA and 22 LMB mines were dropped.

However, this magnetic mine offensive had already begun to fail as early as 22 November, when an He 115 of Kü.Fl.Gr. 106 engaged on a night minelaying mission was startled by anti-aircraft machine-gun fire near Shoeburyness and prematurely dropped its LMA mine in the mudflats of the estuary, from where it was recovered, defused and studied; British counter-measures were soon put into place.

Minelaying was the most effective weapon in the Kriegsmarine arsenal in the war's early months, though unpopular with crews. Here an EMC contact mine is manhandled over the stern. With a warhead of 300kg of explosives, they could be laid in water up to 500m deep. Minelaying's unpopularity with crewmen was mainly due to the inherent danger of potential premature detonation, the frequent proximity of the enemy coast and lack of any tangible results. (Author's collection)

HOW THE FLEET OPERATED

ORGANIZATION
High Naval Command and the *Marinegruppenkommando*

The organization of Kriegsmarine forces in the west was a confusing interplay of offices that dealt with various facets of the war, from operational combat control to the logistics of shore facilities. This organizational structure remained in a near-constant state of evolution throughout the war, though the scope of this study concentrates on the years 1939 to 1942. On 1 June 1935 German naval command had been designated OKM, occupying offices within the Bendlerblock on the Tirpitzufer facing Berlin's Landwehr Canal. *Grossadmiral* Erich Raeder held the position of Commander-in-Chief of the Navy (*Oberbefehlshaber der Kriegsmarine*) and as such headed OKM until his resignation in 1943. Immediately subordinate to Raeder was the Naval War Command; the *Seekriegsleitung*, shortened to SKL. This was the operational 'brain' of the navy, a combined planning and operations department with an integral intelligence division. By the outbreak of war, *Admiral* Otto Schniewind occupied the post of Chief of Staff of the SKL.

It was the SKL which was in direct control of Atlantic surface forces and their supporting units. Correspondingly, Raeder recognized that the complexities of the Atlantic war would make the handling of other geographical spheres of combat extremely difficult. As a result of pre-war studies, an extra layer of command was inserted immediately below SKL, the *Marinegruppenkommando* (MGK). Initially, there were two such offices – MGK West and MGK East – each controlling all Kriegsmarine forces within its designated region of responsibility. This included security forces such as patrol boats, minesweepers of all types and submarine hunters that were used to safeguard German convoy traffic and the coastal approaches to ports and harbours. Responsibility for the collation and dissemination of intelligence information supplied by Luftwaffe maritime units or the B-Dienst radio listening service to all their assigned vessels at sea was also given to the Naval Group Commands. *Marinegruppenkommando Ost* (East) was the first to be created in October 1938, under the command of *Admiral* Conrad Albrecht, a former World War I torpedo boats and destroyer flotilla commander. *Marinegruppenkommando West* only came into being in August 1939, command given to *Admiral* Alfred Saalwächter, an experienced officer who had entered the Imperial Navy in 1910, his service having included two years as a U-boat commander during the previous war. His geographical sphere of concern in 1939 included the North Sea and the Skagerrak as well as the Atlantic approaches, both at the eastern end of the English Channel and north of Britain between the Faroes and Norway.

Previous to the establishment of the Naval Group Commands, the Fleet Commander (*Flottenchef*), *Admiral* Hermann Boehm, had operated independently immediately below SKL level. However, the insertion of MGK West between these two hierarchical levels allowed a more cohesive operational planning structure to be put into place, overseen by officers considered to be thoroughly familiar with all local conditions.

During September 1939, after contrasting viewpoints between the *Flottenchef* and MGK West, SKL issued memorandum that cemented the issue of naval control within the North Sea area, firmly instructing that 'all offensive warfare and the operational use of Fleet forces, even in the Skagerrak and Kattegat, must remain the task of Commanding Admiral, *Marinegruppenkommando West*, and thus be subject to one single authority'.[4] Nonetheless, friction continued between MGK West and the Fleet Commander over where final authority lay.

Following the fall of mainland western Europe to the Wehrmacht in 1940, the Kriegsmarine now controlled a coastline that stretched from the northern reaches of Norway to the Franco–Spanish border. Saalwächter was given responsibility for planning the abortive Operation *Sealion* invasion of Britain and it was decided by SKL that MGK West's operational area would have to be completely refocussed in support of this primary task. Correspondingly, MGK West transferred from Sengwarden to Paris in August 1940, occupying the ex-French Navy Ministry building on Place de la Concorde during

---

4   SKL War Diary, 18 September 1939.

GERMAN BASES IN THE NETHERLANDS, BELGIUM AND FRANCE (overleaf)

The occupation of western Europe stretched existing Kriegsmarine resources while allowing access to conquered port and harbour installations, engineering plants, captured military vessels and a pool of potential civilian craft that could be requisitioned and repurposed.

With Kriegsmarine command and control hierarchy in an almost constant state of evolution throughout the war, this map shows a snapshot of the organizational structure at the beginning of 1941.

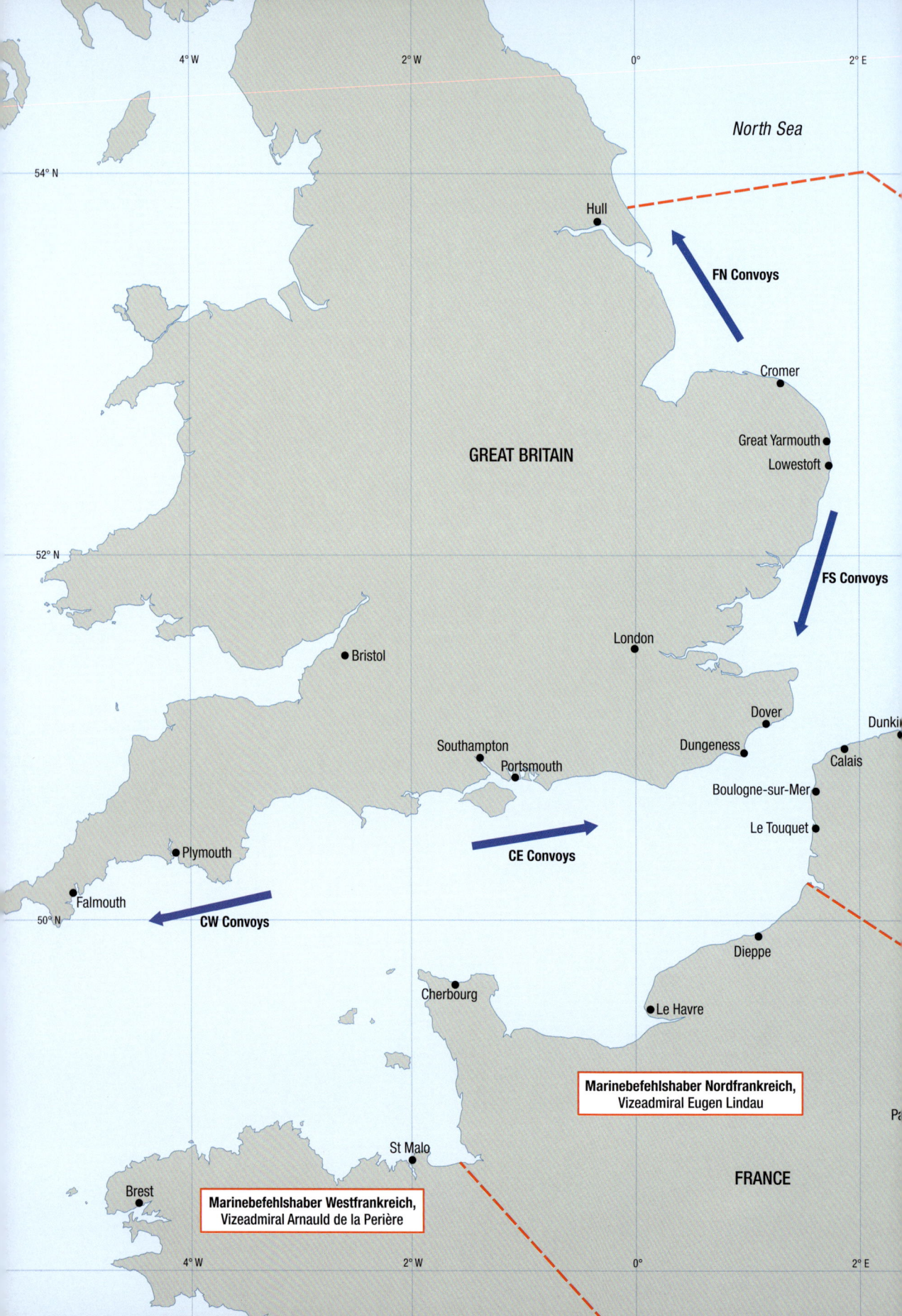

August 1940 to take direct command of all Kriegsmarine units within France and Belgium. This theoretically enabled the easiest level of cooperation with the Army units earmarked for the invasion of Britian while maintaining proper communications and command channels between all naval commands involved, particularly between SKL and MGK West. In the North Sea, MGK East was disbanded and the new MGK North established to take over its previous tasks and those of Saalwächter's staff; the delineation between MGK West and MGK North now lying along a line stretching from southern Greenland to the Outer Hebrides in the north and Den Helder and Cromer in the south. Luftwaffe maritime units and U-boats remained operationally independent, though duty bound to honour deployment requests by Naval Groups.

Marinegruppenkommando North

Generaladmiral Rolf Carls established his new MGK North command in August 1940 in Saalwächter's old headquarters at Sengwarden. Previously, Carls had been the commanding officer of MGK East since October 1939, having replaced the retiring Albrecht. Initially, Carls had remained tasked with Baltic operations until the hierarchy restructuring that followed the fall of France, whereupon Carls became fully responsible for North Sea operations.

However, the existing demarcation line between MGK West and North caused jurisdictional problems regarding offensive action against convoys to and from the Thames estuary. With the boundary line located at Cromer, Carls wanted to operate within this border area, particularly using S-boats. He recommended the relocation of the sector break to the west. However, SKL agreed with the strong opinion expressed by *Kommodore* Friedrich Bonte, who as *Führer der Torpedoboote* (Torpedo Boat Leader, F.d.T.) was responsible for destroyer, torpedo boat and S-boat operations. Bonte urged SKL not to divide S-boat strength between the two *Marinegruppenkommando* as it would lessen the cohesion of operations against convoy traffic bound to and from the Thames. Swayed by his reasoning, the boundary moved north in November 1940, now following a dog-leg from Den Helder to Hull.

Though disappointed by this decision, Carls was somewhat mollified by the transfer to his control of a single S-boat flotilla for other east coast operations.

Carls' Chief of Staff was *Konteradmiral* Otto Klüber, an experienced torpedo boats officer and veteran of the last war. Originally Naval Group North comprised six departments headed by Staff Officers (*Admiralstabsoffizier*) as well as a U-boat liaison officer, Chief Engineering Officer and Medical officer. The departments in August 1940 were:

Rolf Carls on an inspection tour while commander of *Marinegruppenkommando* North. Carls had served aboard SMS *Goeben* during World War I and took part in the Dardenelles campaign before returning to Germany in 1917 and retraining as a U-boat commander. He was captain of U124 at the end of the war. Retiring from active duty in May 1943, he was killed in an RAF raid on the Schleswig-Holstein town of Bad Oldesloe on 24 April 1945 while taking shelter in the cellar of a vocational school. (National Digital Archive, Poland)

1. *Admiralstabsoffizier* (A1 or Asto 1) *Kapitän zur See* Max Freymadl (operations)
2. *Admiralstabsoffizier* (A2) *Korvettenkapitän* Alfred Gohrbrandt (logistics)
3. *Admiralstabsoffizier* (A3) *Korvettenkapitän* Karl-Adolf Zenker (security forces)
4. *Admiralstabsoffizier* (A4) *Kapitän zur See* Max Kupfer (intelligence and communications)
5. *Admiralstabsoffizier* (A5) *Kapitän zur See* Alexander Winther (responsible for the war diary)
6. *Admiralstabsoffizier* (A6) *Korvettenkapitän* Lemelsen (radar)

U-*Admiralstabsoffizier Korvettenkapitän* Max Lemelsen

Gruppen Engineering Officer: *Konteradmiral* (Ing.) Walter Kühn

Chief Medical Officer: *Flottenarzt* Dr Kurt Sander

COMMAND
Kriegsmarine commands in France

Within occupied France, the office of *Kommandierender Admiral West* was established on 27 May 1940, renamed *Kommandierender Admiral Frankreich* on 22 June. This office answered to MGK West and, like Saalwächter and his staff, was also situated in Paris, headed initially by *Admiral* Karlgeorg Schuster, an experienced career officer who had entered the Imperial Navy in 1906. Schuster was principally in charge of personnel administration and troop supply as well as immediately mapping the future use of French naval installations by the Kriegsmarine and overseeing the beginning of construction work for the coastal defence system within the newly occupied territory.

The next step down the pyramidal hierarchy was Naval Commander Northern France (*Marinebefehlshaber Nordfrankreich*), established in Boulogne-sur-Mer under *Vizeadmiral* Eugen Lindau in May 1940. As part of the constant shifting of command lineage, in July 1940 the north-eastern part of Lindau's jurisdiction was separated to create Naval Commander Channel Coast (*Marinebefehlshaber Kanalküste*), *Vizeadmiral* Wilhelm Fleischer, responsible for German naval interests stretching from the Dutch–Belgian border to the mouth of the River Somme. Initially based in Wimille, north of Boulogne-sur-Mer, Fleischer's responsibilities included the French Channel coast east of the Somme estuary and the Belgian coast, except for Antwerp that was under the control of the Commanding Admiral in The Netherlands.

These two separate command entities – Channel Coast and Northern France – were amalgamated in February 1941 when the office of the Naval Commander Northern France was dissolved

German destroyers at sea. The lead ship appears to be rolling heavily in a relatively low swell, demonstrating the inherent instability of the top-heavy destroyers. The apparent advantage of carrying a formidable weapon load was paid for in terms of seaworthiness, as the hull was too slim to maintain stability. (Author's collection)

and Fleischer's Channel Coast office became responsible for territory as far west as the mouth of the Rance near St Malo. From there onwards, naval Commander Atlantic Coast (*Marinebefehlshaber Atlantikküste*) covered the littoral territory between St Malo and the Franco–Spanish border.

The Netherlands had briefly been under MGK West control when the office of Naval Commander Netherlands–Belgium (*Marinebefehlshaber Niederland–Belgien*) had been formed in May 1940 after the German occupation. However, this post was dissolved relatively swiftly and replaced by Naval Commander of The Netherlands (*Marinebefehlshaber in den Niederland*) in June 1940, a post occupied by *Konteradmiral* Helmuth Kienast until July 1942, headquartered in The Hague-Scheveningen. Interestingly, Kienast's command included several riverine flotillas, including the Rhine Flotilla, the Maas Flotilla and, briefly, the Danube Flotilla, all tasked with securing Dutch and Belgian coastal waters, canals and inland waterways.

Marinestation/*Marineoberkommando*

Immediately below the *Marinegruppenkommando* in the hierarchy was the 'Naval Region Command' – originally known as *Marinestation*, but redesignated *Marineoberkommando* (MOK) in the spring of 1943. This post became the most senior *shore* command in any given geographical area, responsible for the administration of all land-based naval assets, including major ports. In total, four naval regions were eventually established in occupied Europe: MOK Baltic; MOK North Sea; MOK South (responsible for the Mediterranean, Adriatic, Aegean and Black Seas); and MOK Norway. In the North Sea, the original *Marinestation der Nordsee* was under the command of *Admiral* Otto Schutze at the outbreak of war, superseded by *Vizeadmiral* Hermann Densch in November 1939.

Cruiser/Destroyer/Torpedo Boat

Kriegsmarine cruisers were the domain of the Commander in Chief Reconnaissance Forces (*Befehlshaber der Aufklärungsstreitkräfte*, or B.d.A.), who was directly subordinate to Fleet Command (*Flottenkommando*), an essentially administrative position with the fleet commander not necessarily in direct control of a fleet at sea, but rather the senior officer to which all major surface ship commanders reported.

However, jurisdictional conflict between a succession of Fleet Commanders and MGK West did not abate until July 1940, with the original contentious issue revolving around the use of minelaying destroyers and light cruisers within the North Sea.

Vizeadmiral Hermann Densch was B.d.A. from September 1937 until October 1939 when he handed over command to *Konteradmiral* Günther Lütjens, becoming Commanding Admiral of North Sea Naval Station (*Marinestation der Nordsee*), which later became MOK North Sea. The heavy cruiser *Admiral Hipper* as well as all light cruisers were the responsibility of the B.d.A., and directly subordinate were the F.d.T. – which held responsibility for destroyers, torpedo

German light cruisers at sea, 1942. (Getty Images)

boats and S-boats – and the minesweepers of all types that were the domain of the Leader of Minesweepers (*Führer der Minensuchboote*, or F.d.M.) *Kapitän zur See* Friedrich Ruge, a torpedo boat veteran of World War I, his office only removed from B.d.A. authority shortly before the outbreak of war.

The duties of the B.d.A. included all human resource management such as selective officer training, the carrying out of all tactical training according to guidelines issued by Fleet Command and assessing all changes in the areas of shipbuilding, mechanical engineering and weapons technology as well as intelligence gathering. Administrative matters specifically assigned to B.d.A. by Fleet Command bypassed the MGK level of authority.

With war imminent in August 1939, the office of F.d.M. was removed from B.d.A. jurisdiction and divided regionally between the two security commands: *Befehlshaber der Sicherung der Ostsee* (Commander in Chief Security Baltic, B.S.O., *Konteradmiral* Hermann Mootz) based in Kiel and *Befehlshaber der Sicherung der Nordsee* (North Sea, B.S.N., *Konteradmiral* Otto von Schrader) quartered aboard the survey ship *Meteor* in Wilhelmshaven. The regional *Befehlshaber der Sicherung* were in turn subordinate to the relevant geographical naval command, such as *Marinegruppenkommando West* or *Nord*.

On 30 October 1939 the existing F.d.T. – *Kapitän zur See* Bonte – was retitled to the new post of *Führer der Zerstörer* (F.d.Z., Commander Destroyers) with all destroyers placed immediately under his command. In Swinemünde, *Kapitän zur See* Hans Bütow was appointed the new F.d.T. with torpedo boat and S-boat flotillas remaining under his command. The reasoning for this restructuring was that long-range operations were extremely rare for torpedo boats or S-boats, and both were considered likely to be frequently requested to carry out localized defensive tasks. It was therefore considered that direct subordination to F.d.Z. would entail an undesirable burden in operational control, as the undertakings and capabilities of destroyers differed fundamentally from those of the smaller torpedo boats. Additionally, the arrival of newly planned torpedo boat flotillas would result in an increased workload with all its potential detrimental effect on destroyers' operational control. S-boats would not receive autonomous command until 20 April 1942, when *Korvettenkapitän* Rudolf Petersen was named *Führer der Schnellboote* (F.d.S.). At that time F.d.S. headquarters remained at Scheveningen from where the F.d.T. was operating and, while Petersen exercised an overall say with all active S-boats, his tactical control only concerned those deployed in the west, thereby remaining within the command sphere of MGK West.

Even some of the pre-1914 vintage torpedo boats returned to Kriegsmarine service after the outbreak of war were used for minelaying. Here men are shown on the stern flak position by their single 2cm anti-aircraft gun. The triple tube torpedo battery is in the foreground. (Author's collection)

On 9 January 1941 *Vizeadmiral* Hermann Mootz vacated his post as B.S.W. to oversee the testing of newly constructed warships, his place briefly taken by *Vizeadmiral* Hermann von Fischel who occupied the chair for a month, during which time the Western Kriegsmarine command structure was drastically altered. The existing B.S.W. staff was dissolved and replaced by men who had previously staffed the offices of F.d.M. West and F.d.V. (*Führer der Vorpostenboote*) West, the latter responsible for patrol boat operations. Installed in Paris, under newly promoted *Vizeadmiral* Ruge's command, the border between B.S.W. and B.S.N. was moved west so that The Netherlands was removed from Ruge's sphere of operations.

The F.d.V. and F.d.M. commands were also fused and Security Divisions (*Sicherungsdivisionen*) established in their stead on 17 February 1941. Each Division was responsible for a sector of coastline and the incumbent work such as the protection of naval bases, requisitioning new vessels, the formation of new flotillas and general convoy protection, minesweeping, minelaying and ASW operations.

Four *Sicherungsdivisionen* were initially created. The 1st *Sicherungsdivision* responsible for The Netherlands and Germany's North Sea coast with its headquarters in The Hague was under the command of *Fregattenkapitän* Heinrich Bramesfeld who built his staff around the existing core of F.d.M. *Niederlande*. *Kapitän zur See* Karl Weniger, previously F.d.M. *Nordfrankreich*, based his new 2nd *Sicherungsdivisionen* in the Château du Souverain-Moulin near Boulogne. His responsibility stretched over an area covering Belgian and northern French coastal waters to Cherbourg, his units based in Bruges, Ostend, Dunkirk, Boulogne-Wimereux, Dieppe, Le Havre, Ouistreham and Cherbourg as well as the British Channel Islands. *Kapitän zur See* Heinz Schiller centred the 3rd *Sicherungsdivision* initially at Brest before moving to Trez Hir near Plougenvelin. His zone stretched from the western portion of the English Channel to the Loire estuary; the primary ports used by his forces being St Malo, Brest, Concarneau, Benodet and Lorient. The final French Atlantic unit, 4th *Sicherungsdivision*, was based at Larmor-Plage near Lorient, *Kapitän zur See* Anselm Lautenschlager responsible for the region between the River Loire and the Spanish frontier, using the ports of Nantes/Coueron, Paimboeuf, Saint Nazaire, Les Sables-d'Olonne, La Pallice, Royan, Pauillac, Bordeaux, Bayonne and Saint Jean-de-Luz.

INTELLIGENCE

The distribution of Britain's warships was already known to the Kriegsmarine at the outbreak of war thanks to the cryptanalysis department of SKL's naval intelligence unit, located in 72–76 Tirpitzufer in Berlin. Known as the *Beobachtungsdienst* – shortened to *B-Dienst* – the department had come into its own in 1935 when one of its most gifted operatives, cryptanalyst Wilhelm Tranow, had broken the Royal Navy's most widely used 5-digit Naval

Administrative Code used to communicate between Royal Navy and merchant shipping. This was comprehensively penetrated until 1943. French cyphers had posed no such problem and been compromised quickly.

B-Dienst personnel numbered only 30 in 1937, but within two years had reached 500 and continued to grow. Initially it was part of an independent department within OKM, headed by *Kapitän zur See* Theodor Arps, and known as the Naval Intelligence Service (*Marinenachrichtendienst*). On 1 October 1937 it was incorporated within 3./SKL, *Kapitän zur See* Heinz Bonatz appointed the head of the B-Dienst subsection, which successfully resisted all attempts by the Wehrmacht's Intelligence Service – the Abwehr – to integrate all signals intelligence beneath its singular control. Each major surface ship carried a small number of B-Dienst personnel aboard; cypher and decoding specialists who could keep the ship's operations officers up to date with the latest intercepted information. A small B-Dienst unit was also permanently stationed at F.d.S. headquarters from 1 August 1942.

The Kriegsmarine quickly established an observation station on Cape Griz-Nez immediately following the fall of France. Initially accommodated in an old bus, it was able to immediately begin reporting shipping movements along the British Channel coast. On 13 July, MGK West called SKL's attention to the importance of this post for operations by both naval and Luftwaffe units, requesting *Admiral* Karlgeorg Schuster as Commanding Admiral, France (*Kommandierender Admiral Frankreich*) supply personnel and equipment 'adequate for operational requirements'. The construction of radar stations and observation bunkers soon began at various points along the Channel coast.

Luftwaffe reports of ship movements were extremely valuable to the Kriegsmarine for planning attacks or indicating where the best potential minefields could be situated. For example, observations reported by bomber crews headed to mainland Britain, of merchant shipping steaming in narrow lanes through declared minefields encouraged the immediate dropping of further mines within those channels. Every time a channel was swept, attempts were made to block it once more. Likewise, with every mine detonation that claimed a victim, there was one less mine forming the intended barrier, needing to be located and replaced if possible. However, the constant tug-of-war between the pragmatic Raeder and Göring's hubris over control of a dedicated maritime air arm resulted in ever-increasing Luftwaffe responsibility for aerial reconnaissance of British naval bases and coastal areas. With no attached naval officers, their maritime navigation was distinctly substandard and therefore the accuracy in sighting reports was frequently unreliable. Göring continually obsessed over the dismantling of the naval air arm and subsuming all aerial forces under his control, thereby robbing the Kriegsmarine of much by way of effective aerial intelligence.

While agents on the ground in such places as Spain and Portugal provided intelligence for some Allied Atlantic convoy traffic, not much

Reichsmarschall Hermann Göring with *Admiral* Carls in Gotenhafen. Head of the Luftwaffe, what Göring lacked as a military leader he compensated for with his adept political manoeuvring. Thanks, in the main, to his short-sighted vanity, the Kriegsmarine was denied an effective fleet air arm that may have influenced coastal operations. (Author's collection)

Hitler with his entourage visiting the island of Heligoland. To the left of Hitler is *Vizeadmiral* Hermann Densch, commander of the North Sea Naval Station. To his right is *Admiral* Alfred Saalwächter, commander of MGK West under whose jurisdiction the North Sea fell until mid-1940. (Interfoto / Alamy Stock Photo)

agent work was received from Britain. Although the Abwehr dropped multiple spies as part of Operation *Lena* before the planned invasion of Britain, their ineptitude was so extreme that some historians now believe their failure intentional. Indeed, many of the highest-level officers within the Abwehr – including its chief *Admiral* Wilhelm Canaris – were committed opponents of the Nazi regime and frequently attempted to undermine operations to bring about the fall of the National Socialist government and hasten the end of the war.

LOGISTICS AND FACILITIES

The primary German port for North Sea deployment was Wilhelmshaven on the Jade Bight, with the fortified harbour on Heligoland 50km into the North Sea also used by S-boats. With the occupation of western Europe in 1940, the Kriegsmarine received a bonanza of ports and harbours stretching the entire length of the Channel and Atlantic coast from which to operate against Britain.

Almost immediately, OKW ordered heavy artillery batteries – both naval and army – established on the French Channel coast for use against Britain. Coastal batteries of both services were seconded to naval command, in this case the responsibility of *Admiral* Schuster as Commanding Admiral, France, who in turn delegated to *Konteradmiral* Wilhelm Fleischer as newly appointed Naval Commander Channel Coast (*Marinebefehlshaber Kanalküste*).

On 16 July, Hitler issued Directive 16 in which he outlined the proposed invasion of Britain, Operation *Seelöwe* (Sealion). He tasked the Kriegsmarine with coordinating the establishment of coastal artillery – and its subsequent fire control – intended to engage targets at sea. He further ordered the largest possible number of extra-heavy guns to be brought into position as soon as possible, to cover any attempted crossing and shield its flanks against enemy naval action. Railway guns were included in this, though those extra-heavy batteries were

PLANNED INVASION ROUTES FOR OPERATION *SEELÖWE* (SEALION)

Operation *Seelöwe* was far beyond Wehrmacht capabilities at that time. With no specialized landing craft – much of the invasion was reliant on barges that would be towed across the Channel – army units would have suffered disproportionate casualties and logistical chaos. Without German dominance in the air, the RAF would be free to hinder any attempted invasion. Finally, and arguably most importantly, after disastrous losses in Norway, the Kriegsmarine would have been virtually powerless to deflect the Royal Navy and Air Force from inflicting severe damage on any potential invasion fleet. Furthermore, keeping an army supplied in the field if it had successfully landed would have been beyond both Kriegsmarine and Luftwaffe capabilities. Nevertheless, much of MGK West's efforts were directed towards *Seelöwe* during the summer of 1940. With Saalwächter in command of naval forces, *Admiral* Günther Lütjens was named naval Commander West for *Seelöwe*.

intended *only* to deal with targets on the English mainland – K5 (28cm) and K12 (21cm) railway guns – were not included within naval responsibility. Major coastal batteries were to be enclosed in concrete, this work was undertaken by the Organization Todt.

Over 9,000 Todt workers were employed building gun emplacements although *Vizeadmiral* Karl Witzel, Chief of the Naval Ordnance Division (*Marinewaffenamt*), was at pains to point out that the Army's railway guns and other motorized batteries were of limited effectiveness due to their wide dispersal, slow traverse speed, long loading time and ammunition shortages. For those same reasons, Witzel stressed, such heavy guns could not substantially support any cross-channel invasion.

Far better suited were the five naval batteries near Calais – heavy calibre yet accurate and with good traverse capabilities. The first, two 28cm guns of *Prinz Heinrich* battery followed by four 28cm guns of battery *Grosser Kurfürst*, were ready for action by August 1940, thanks to the herculean effort of the Todt engineers and labourers. The remaining three large naval batteries capable of harassing fire against British coastal convoys were all operational by mid-September. Fire control was provided by both reconnaissance aircraft and multiple radar stations capable of detecting craft as small as MTBs. Among other smaller batteries in their charge, men of *Korvettenkapitän* Fritz Diekmann's MAA (*Marine Artillerie Abteilung*) 240 manned one of the five large batteries – *Friedrich August* (30.5cm) – *Korvettenkapitän* Kurt Schilling's MAA 242 two batteries – *Grosser Kurfürst* (28cm) and *Siegfried* (38cm) – while *Korvettenkapitän* Hans Stührenberg's MAA 244 held the last two – *Prinz Heinrich* (28cm) and *Oldenburg* (24cm). In July 1940 *Kapitän zur See* Julius Steinbach was appointed Naval Artillery Commander for the Pas de Calais region, which expanded to include Flanders in September 1941, centralizing overall control of the regional coastal artillery.

Though this may be seen as the genesis of the vaunted 'Atlantic Wall', construction of that ambitious fortification of the entire German-occupied coastline stretching from northern Norway to the Franco–Spanish border did not begin in earnest until after 23 March 1942 when Hitler issued Directive 40 which detailed plans for the fortification project.

Following the surrender of The Netherlands, *Schnellboote* were moved to the Dutch harbours of Den Helder and the Hook of Holland during May as soon as Allied mines had been cleared and damage to harbour installations repaired. This greatly reduced transit times to the front line and after the fall of Belgium and France, S-boats were immediately established in Boulogne and Cherbourg.

Raeder had initially denied requests to fortify the Dutch harbours with protective S-boat shelters, but soon relented as the flotillas established themselves and British harassing air attacks began. The Organization Todt began constructing sheltered docks and associated workshops and weaponry stores in Ijmuiden, Rotterdam, Ostend, Boulogne and Cherbourg as the threat of enemy air attack increased dramatically following the end of the Battle of Britain. On 10 June 1940, the first four berths in Ostend were declared operational. Eleven days later, Boulogne's bunker was also operational: Rotterdam following in October and Ijmuiden early in 1942. In Cherbourg, existing berths were covered with a vault of steel-reinforced concrete and declared useable at the beginning of 1941. The Boulogne bunker could accommodate 12 S-boats and had a torpedo bunker situated immediately to the rear with railway track access for both bringing new torpedoes in and transferring them to the boats in their berths. Unlike the U-boat bunkers that had taken priority along the Atlantic coast, those that would house the S-boats (and often R-boats) had a roof thickness of only 200cm and were felt to be sufficient against enemy bombing at that stage of the war. The consequence of neglecting to strengthen these defences only became obvious in 1944 when RAF Lancaster bombers struck with Tallboy bombs, destroying several S-boats.

Germany made full use of major harbours as well as minor ports and anchorages within the occupied territories. German coastal convoys generally travelled in small bounds between sheltered ports to maximize defences provided by local security units and coastal artillery. Here a German sailor observes French fishing boats from his artillery harbour defence position. (DPA Picture Alliance / Alamy Stock Photo)

Various occupied harbours were allocated as main supporting stations for different vessel types. For example, Boulogne was rated as a supply point for destroyers, S-boats, R-boats and *Vorpostenboote*, while Le Havre was designated for 'all light craft up to destroyers'.[5] Supplying the harbours within occupied territories proved a logistical challenge for the Kriegsmarine and, with limited railway rolling stock and damaged portions of transport infrastructure through occupied territories, merchant ships were heavily utilized. These required convoying and an escort from Germany, and became a target for RAF Coastal Command as well as the Royal Navy. The former experienced little initial success with 161 aircraft lost for the sinking of only six ships and another 14 damaged, predominantly in and around convoys from Norway to Germany, during 1940. Outdated equipment, lacklustre intelligence, poor serviceability of machines, low morale and a lack of cohesive tactical method had combined to defeat Coastal Command efforts. Correspondingly, *Vorpostenboote*, *U-Boot Jäger* and *Sperrbrecher* escorts provided effective protection; collectively known to the Allies as 'flak ships'. Eventually, the heavily armed flak ships became targets themselves, experimenting with towed barrage balloons and on-board flamethrowers, to differing degrees of success.

However, after the British Admiralty's assumption of control of Coastal Command, more suitable machines such as Beauforts and Beaufighters were put into action and fortunes improved during 1941. The cipher used by German and German-occupied dockyards as well as small patrol craft that did not carry Enigma machines, known as *Werftschlüssel*, was broken in February 1941, providing the British with intelligence from signals traffic alerting dockyards of convoy departure and arrival times. Luftwaffe Enigma codes had also been broken; particularly important for convoy traffic escorted by fighters and thus betraying its value to Coastal Command. Finally, from August 1941, Kriegsmarine Enigma was regularly broken, providing exact German convoy information and leading to ever increasingly effective attacks.

---

5   MGK West organizational document, 10 July 1940.

COMBAT AND ANALYSIS

THE FLEET IN COMBAT
1939

When Germany attacked Poland on 1 September, most Kriegsmarine surface forces were stationed within the Baltic Sea, with MGK West allocated a smattering of security units and a single S-boat flotilla. The Polish Navy was, however, quickly neutralized and by 3 September, when Britain and France declared war on Germany, the Baltic Kriegsmarine surface presence was disproportionately large and vulnerable to the sole remaining threat of Polish submarines. Thus, *Vizeadmiral* Hermann Densch, B.d.A., aboard his flagship *Nürnberg* led his four light cruisers – *Nürnberg*, *Königsberg*, *Leipzig* and *Köln* – into the North Sea where they were placed at the disposal of MGK West. They were soon followed by 1st Destroyer Flotilla, 5th Destroyer Division and 1st S-Flotilla. Furthermore, three Type VII U-boats of the designated *Schweden* group were placed at Saalwächter's disposal after having abortively patrolled north of Hela hunting for Poland's tiny navy. More U-boats would be seconded to MGK West control; tasked with Operation *Ulla* that had initially involved reconnaissance of the eastern English Channel and Thames estuary, it was expanded to minelaying. At this stage of the war, U-boat command had not yet achieved any form of autonomy and it remained very much under the control of more senior offices, such as the *Marinegruppenkommando*.

With the stage now set to commence North Sea operations against Britain, immediate moves were defensive with extensive minelaying of the 'Westwall' barrier designed to safeguard the Heligoland Bight and stretching from the island of Borkum to Limfjord on the Jutland peninsula. For much of September, 16 destroyers laid Westwall mines in conjunction with the minelayers *Grille*, *Roland* and *Cobra* and three of Densch's light cruisers (*Königsberg* having returned to the Baltic for gunnery exercises). Apart from a loading accident aboard destroyer *Z10 Hans Lody* that killed two men and wounded six others, the minelaying was undertaken without loss.

Within the North Sea the Royal Navy also began laying a mine barrage from Dover to the Orkneys. Between 20 and 50 miles wide, narrow convoy lanes were left between the mines and coastline. Relatively small fields of both deep and shallow mines were initially laid until increased mine stocks allowed a more extensive east coast mine barrier to be established from December onwards. Over 6,000 mines were also planted across the Dover Strait in an echo of the World War I Dover Barrage that had effectively sealed off the English Channel for U-boats by 1918. Naturally, each side also began offensive minelaying in any transit channels detected in enemy fields, and though both sides obeyed Hague Convention rules and declared mined areas, Raeder noted that Britain had placed its merchant shipping within convoys protected by armed escorts. Pedantically, but correctly, this meant that *strictly commercial* trade routes to British ports no longer existed and therefore Article 2 of the Hague Convention forbidding the use of mines 'with the sole object of intercepting commercial shipping' no longer applied.

The light cruiser *Königsberg*, in 1936. Launched on 26 March 1927, *Königsberg* had entered Reichsmarine service in April 1929 to replace the obsolete turn-of-the-century *Thetis*, a remnant of the Imperial German Navy. The cruiser took part in North Sea minelaying of the 'Westwall' barrage and was sunk during the early stages of the invasion of Norway. (Ajax News & Feature Service / Alamy Stock Photo)

On 18 September 1939, Saalwächter informed SKL that major Fleet vessels were not yet ready for offensive action, requiring increased combat training. Coincidently, Luftwaffe reconnaissance reported few worthwhile targets for heavy forces in the North Sea. However, he proposed surprise operations by destroyers against merchant shipping reported sailing independently from the Skagerrak to Britain in defiance of the declared blockade. He intended to amass at least ten destroyers and reasoned that, if this thrust caused enemy convoy formation, then a favourable target would then exist for heavy units.

Saalwächter also lobbied SKL repeatedly for confirmation that MGK West would remain the sole authority for all operational deployment of Fleet forces in the North Sea, as well as the Skagerrak and Kattegat. He wanted to remove confusion over whose authority achieved precedence and to avoid the unexpected logistical difficulties caused when Fleet forces were allocated elsewhere and returned in unknown states of readiness. To the chagrin of the *Flottenchef Vizeadmiral* Wilhelm Marschall, Saalwächter was granted overall authority, thereby leaving the former feeling that he had been robbed of the freedom of action while at sea with his ships.

Unwilling to await ten destroyers' readiness, SKL urged Saalwächter to mount his destroyer thrusts without delay, so the first were despatched northward from

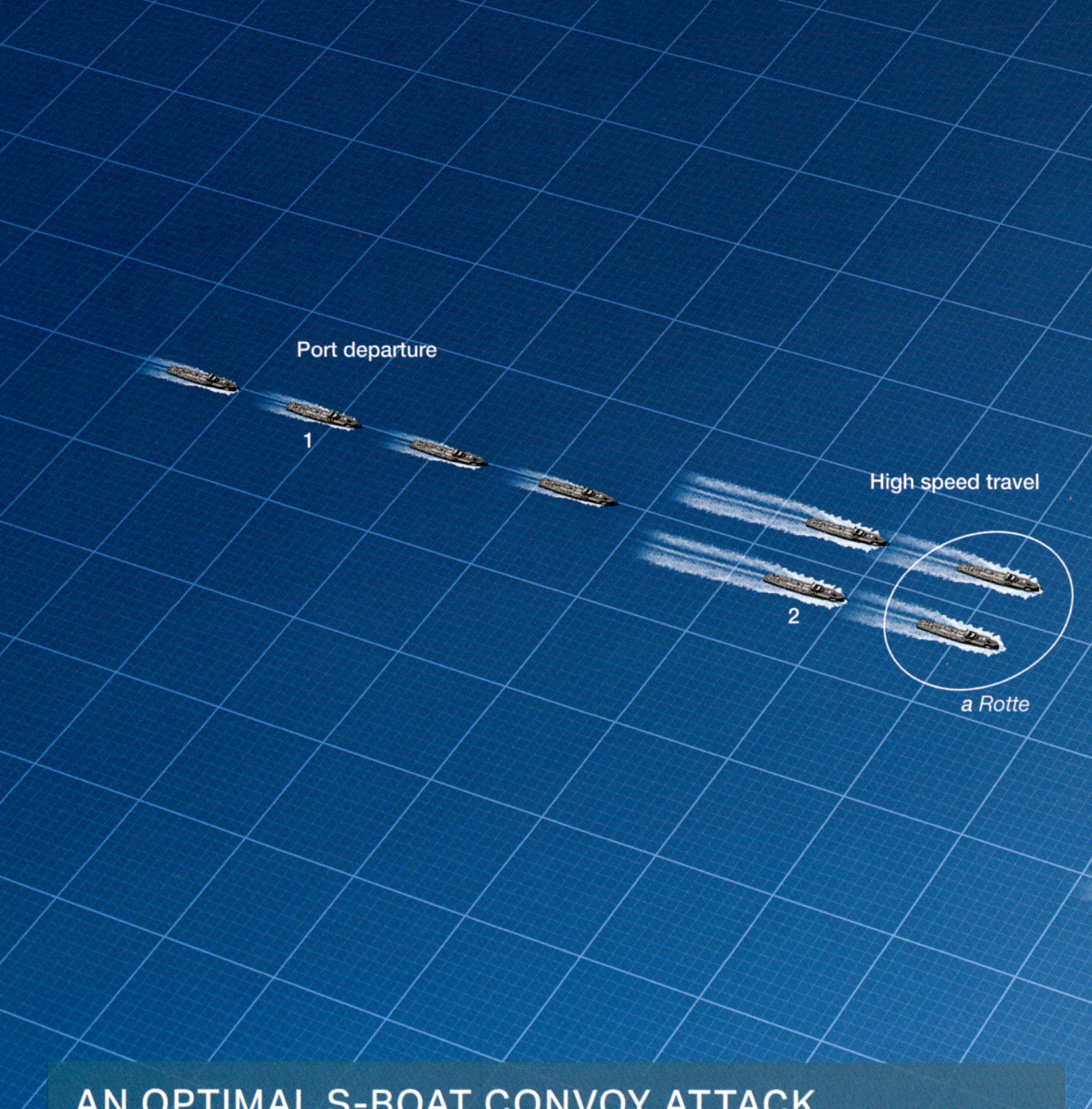

AN OPTIMAL S-BOAT CONVOY ATTACK

Although S-boat operations were highly dependent on both serviceability affecting available numbers and weather conditions, an optimal convoy attack utilized the *Lauertaktik*. This method comprised three distinct phases. Seldom working alone, S-boats usually attacked in pairs (a *Rotte*) or larger numbers, remaining in visual contact after leaving harbour for as long as possible and then continuing to pass any necessary signals via VHF radio, which would soon prove detrimental to operations as the Allies used German-speaking 'headache' operators to follow S-boat operations at sea.

The first phase (1) was the departure from port of S-boats travelling in line ahead formation. Once midway to their target area they would accelerate to high speed in their *Rotten* (2), each still travelling in line ahead. Once near the target (3) each *Rotte* would decelerate and spread out along the expected convoy path leaving one nautical mile between them. Often lying stationary in wait, they would accelerate to the attack, launch torpedoes and immediately peel away to left and right and retreat, either to reload or return to base, avoiding counter-attacking if at all possible.

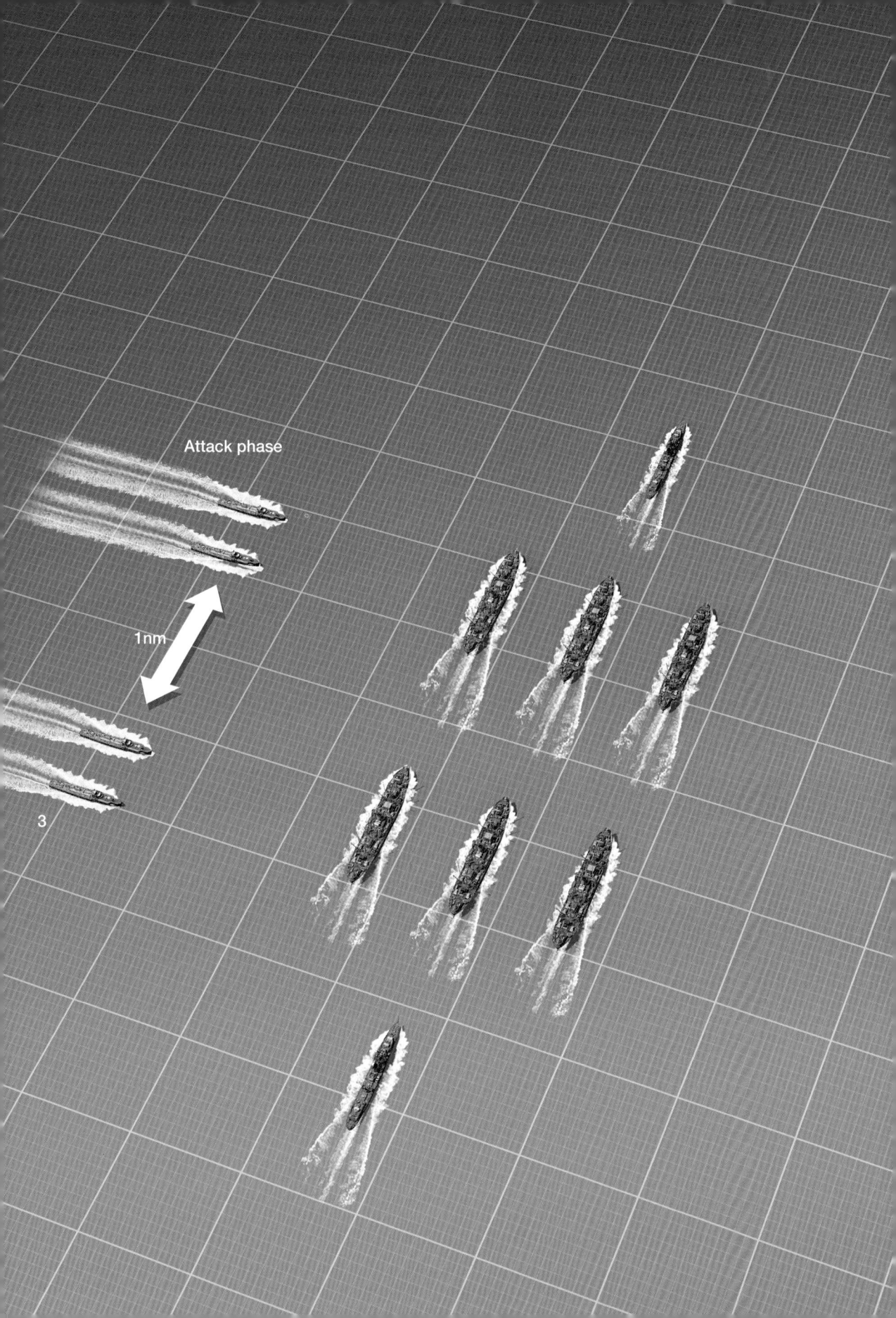

Wilhelmshaven on 26 September. The originally planned drive into the central North Sea had been modified under orders from SKL to instead focus on the Skagerrak entrance. Under direct command of F.d.T. *Konteradmiral* Lütjens aboard *Z21 Wilhelm Heidkamp*, by 1 October they had stopped and searched 104 merchant ships; 13 had been seized and taken to a German port, deemed to be carrying contraband. As a result of this stringent intervention, Danish export trade to Britain was paralysed.

Unfortunately, deteriorating weather posed significant problems for the German destroyers, the delicate and largely untried steam propulsion plants of which proved unmatched to the rigours of short-sharp wartime operations. Saalwächter himself requested the destroyers be replaced by fast *Vorpostenboote* for the stop and search operations, but he was overruled. Likewise, S-boats within the North Sea were being used for purposes to which they were ill suited. The S-boats patrolled the German Bight providing security for larger ships or operating as submarine hunters, neither of which tasks suited this type of vessel. The low bridge of an S-boat yielded a near horizon and spotting enemy periscopes or torpedo tracks at any usable distance was almost impossible. Despite carrying depth charges, ASW work was wholly unfitting and in months to come, depth charges were frequently fitted with floats to delay their descent and instead used as a means of deterring surface pursuit. Escorting slower ships meant that the S-boats were sailing well below their planned operational speeds, generally using only the central engine with increased strain placed upon it, requiring more frequent overhauls and repairs. Naval High Command had little concept of how to utilize their S-boats to full advantage and, coupled with planned operations curtailed through worsening winter conditions, this resulted in a seemingly ineffective service. In November Saalwächter went as far as to claim that S-boat groups had 'fallen short of expectations in every respect', a sentiment that resulted in plans to limit the construction of new boats. It was an inauspicious start to S-boat combat service.

Heavy units were first sortied into the North Sea on the evening of 7 October when battleship *Gneisenau* and light cruiser *Köln* sailed from the Jade Bight into the North Sea, accompanied by destroyers *Z21 Wilhelm Heidkamp*, *Z14 Friedrich Ihn*, *Z17 Diether von Roeder*, *Z20 Karl Galster*, *Z6 Theodor Riedel*, *Z3 Max Schultz*, *Z11 Bernd von Arnim* and *Z16 Friedrich Eckoldt*. Their mission was threefold: to supplement the war against merchant shipping in the Skagerrak by a thrust into an area where enemy escort activities may perhaps be expected; to relieve pressure on German pocket battleships in the Atlantic by leading the enemy to believe another break through into the North Atlantic was being attempted, thus preventing further Royal Navy or French battle cruisers being sent to the Atlantic; and lastly to lure British forces from their bases, giving the Luftwaffe and U-boats an opportunity to attack.

This latter objective was confirmed as successful by B-Dienst, which had identified the 1st British Battleship Squadron, so 2nd Cruiser Squadron and destroyers of the 6th and 7th Destroyer Flotillas all headed out to intercept.

The Luftwaffe mounted its largest maritime hunt thus far, though results obtained were negligible. Weaknesses in nautical navigation among the conventional Luftwaffe crews had rendered sighting reports wildly inaccurate, a problem compounded by poor weather conditions, which soon reduced the Luftwaffe component to a shambles. Three separately identified Royal Navy groups transpired to be just one that had been reported in various locations, owing to imprecise navigation.

German destroyers in action. (National Digital Archive, Poland)

No concerted Luftwaffe attack was mounted, though small groups attempted to bomb sporadically, and erroneous reports of success were received by wireless in Germany. Meanwhile, *Gneisenau* and its accompanying ships returned safely to port unmolested.

On 17 October F.d.T. Lütjens aboard *Heidkamp* led five destroyers laden with 90 RMA and 90 RMB magnetic ground mines to begin minelaying in British waters. Their first sortie concentrated between the Humber estuary and Withernsea Light and was carried out undetected and without incident. In a pattern repeated for each minelaying mission, the destroyers feinted north towards Norway lest they be observed by enemy reconnaissance and their destination deduced, before crossing west from the Skagerrak entrance across the North Sea under cover of darkness, returning via the same route. Five days after this initial minefield had been laid, 1,692 GRT British steamer SS *Whitemantle* of London's Gas Light & Coke Company carrying coal from the River Tyne to London detonated a mine east of Withernsea Light and sank with all 14 crew killed. It was the first of seven ships totalling 25,825 GRT that would be lost to this minefield. Destroyers carried out a total of 11 minelaying sorties by February 1940, sailing during full-moon periods, sowing extensive minefields in the shallow inshore waters between Newcastle upon Tyne and the Thames estuary. British port operations were severely hampered with shipping channels repeatedly closed after discoveries of mines. A total of 76 merchant vessels were confirmed sunk by destroyer-laid mines between 22 October 1939 and 12 March 1940, totalling 258,465 GRT of merchant shipping. The largest victim was 14,294 GRT Polish troop transport MV *Pilsudski* sunk on 26 November with ten crew killed, the smallest was the 81 GRT trawler *Eta* that snagged a mine in its net on 6 January near the Outer Gabbard light ship in the Thames estuary, though all crewmen successfully abandoned ship. A further five freighters were damaged.

SS *Whitemantle* of London's Gas Light & Coke Company, sunk on 22 October 1939 while carrying coal from the River Tyne to London. The first ship sunk by destroyer-laid mines off the British east coast. (Author's collection)

Although convoying was instituted on this coastal route in 1939 – the first sailing from Firth of Forth for London on 6 September 1939 – Royal Navy reports from the Rosyth Escort Force, in whose care they were placed, lamented the ability of the small coastal steamers to form organized convoys, noting a shocking lack of station keeping. Those convoys that were successfully formed frequently straggled at night and many ships remained sailing independently, suffering disproportionate losses from mines. The Admiralty's official history later noted that three out of every four ships sunk in British coastal waters were sailing alone.

In addition to the merchant losses, HMS *Blanche* was sunk – the first destroyer lost to German action – as well as the destroyer HMS *Grenville*, with minelaying cruiser HMS *Adventure* being badly damaged. Fortunately for the British, such German destroyer sorties were also regularly cancelled or reduced in strength, due to frequent problems with the temperamental steam turbines. Operational readiness was severely impacted; a report of 9 November revealed that eight destroyers were temporarily out of commission and undergoing repairs. Indeed, a massed destroyer operation planned against the British fishing fleet south of the Dogger Bank planned for early December was indefinitely postponed due to a poor state of destroyer readiness.

Destroyer minelaying missions involved at least one destroyer acting as escort to the others engaged in minelaying. To bolster protection, light cruisers were allocated to rendezvous with the destroyers once minelaying was complete, providing potential fire support for their return to base. This was essentially a role-reversal for destroyers that were intended to screen larger ships, Saalwächter already having turned down plans to use battleships as distant support. He believed that heavy forces used in this way would be exposed to unnecessary danger from enemy aircraft and submarines. Their presence was also likely to eliminate the element of surprise from the minelaying operations, the destroyers' best protection being their unexpected appearance and speed. Instead, he advocated that aircraft be used to provide such cover. Ultimately, though battleships were never thus employed, light cruisers were and Saalwächter was to be proved correct in his main point of contention during December.

As minelaying continued, German and British destroyers clashed for the first time. On the morning of 6 December *Fregattenkapitän* Erich Bey took three ships of 4th Destroyer Flotilla – *Z10 Hans Lody* (acting as escort with Bey aboard), *Z11 Bernd von Arnim* and *Z12 Erich Giese* (carrying 5 RMAs, 26 RMBs and 110 moored mines between them) – from Wilhelmshaven for a minelaying mission off Cromer Light. In an inauspicious start, *Bernd von Arnim* experienced burst boiler tubes, forcing it to abort the mission and return to Wilhelmshaven.

Bey pressed on and reached the planned position a little after 0200hrs on calm seas, under a clear starlit night. Two darkened ships were seen approaching a little after midnight, though they reversed course and disappeared before coming too close. These were the destroyers HMS *Jersey* and *Juno* patrolling the waters between the Humber and Outer Dowsing and they had failed to detect the approaching Germans. At 0212hrs *Erich Giese* began laying its 76 mines and despite two premature detonations which startled the crew, completed the task in less than half an hour as *Hans Lody* stood off to the north providing cover. Two ships would later be sunk by these mines.

Bey then led the destroyers north to circumnavigate sandbanks before turning east and the same two darkened ships were sighted running almost parallel about 8,000m distant. They were soon identified as destroyers through *Hans Lody*'s gun sights and Bey ordered course fractionally changed and speed increased to maximum, the two German destroyers slowly converging on the British ships which were travelling at 26kts and had not sighted their enemy.

By 0310hrs, the distance had closed to 4,600m, and four minutes later, leading ship *Hans Lody* fired three torpedoes at HMS *Juno* while *Erich Giese* fired four at HMS *Jersey*. Both Germans then sheared off to the east. It appears that the 3m depth settings for *Hans Lody*'s torpedoes was too deep for *Juno*'s shallow draught and they all missed. However, one from *Erich Giese* hit *Jersey* on its port side in the fuel bunkers, starting a major fire that threw sheets of flame skyward, clearly visible aboard the retreating German ships. Ten crewmen were killed and others were trapped in the ship's stern until rescued by the whaler *Juno*, which immediately moved to assist while laying smoke.

The German attackers remained undetected, a U-boat was believed to be responsible for the torpedo

A German destroyer burying its nose in moderate sea; a recurrent design problem. (Naval History and Heritage Command)

The light cruiser *Köln*. The third of the Königsberg class to be built, *Köln* laid part of the Westwall mine barrier, took part in sorties alongside battleships and was the only light cruiser not damaged by submarine attack after acting as cover for destroyers returning from minelaying off the British east coast in December 1939. From late 1940, it was moved to the Baltic fleet and thereafter Norway, from where it operated until sunk in harbour by USAAF bombing on 30 March 1945. (Getty Images)

and, as Bey believed *Jersey* was sinking with the entire stern blown off, he opted not to engage in gun action or attempt further torpedo attacks and continued to Wilhelmshaven. Though HMS *Jersey* did not sink, it was towed into the Humber and would require ten months of repairs before being operational again. Both British and German press attributed the attack to a U-boat; OKM not wanting to draw attention to destroyer operations so close inshore to the British mainland.

The next minelaying operation took place on the night of 12 December. *Kapitän zur See* Helmut Bonte, F.d.Z., led the foray aboard *Z19 Hermann Künne* as escort to four minelaying destroyers (*Z15 Erich Steinbrinck*, *Z8 Bruno Heinemann*, *Z14 Friedrich Ihn* and *Z4 Richard Beitzen*), each of which carried 60 moored contact mines. They were scheduled to lay their mines off Newcastle at the northern border of a flanking British minefield. Meanwhile, the newly appointed B.d.A. *Konteradmiral* Lütjens sailed in a holding pattern with cruisers *Nürnberg*, *Leipzig* and *Köln* on the eastern fringe of the North Sea to rendezvous with the returning destroyers.

The mines were dropped accurately as British coastal lights in the Tyne area were inexplicably still burning, enabling strong navigational fixes. As the destroyers left the area at high speed for rendezvous with the light cruisers, a sudden fire in *Bruno Heinemann*'s No.2 turbine room brought the ship to an unwelcome stop, with *Erich Steinbrinck* standing by as cover for over an hour as firefighting units quelled the flames. Meanwhile, disaster overwhelmed Lütjens at 1124hrs when a torpedo impacted the waiting *Leipzig* amidships, destroying the forward boiler room. Undetected, submarine HMS *Salmon* had been stalking the three zig-zagging cruisers – misidentified as *Blücher*, *Leipzig* and *Admiral Hipper* – for nearly two hours. A full bow salvo of six torpedoes was fired at the two rearmost ships, at a range estimated to be 5,000yds, just as a pair of escorting Heinkel He 115 floatplanes arrived overhead. As *Leipzig* reeled from the impact, Lütjens ordered all ships immediately steer 90° to starboard, and aboard *Nürnberg* two torpedo tracks were spotted that would hit the starboard flank if the turn continued. *Kapitän zur See* Otto Klüber ordered full opposite rudder, and one passed harmlessly ahead of the ship, but the second struck her in the bow, tearing away the entire stem. *Nürnberg* reduced speed to 12kts to allow damage assessment; more tracks were spotted to port, but *Nürnberg* increased speed leaving them to explode in its wake. Though experiencing minor flooding, the damage was slight and watertight bulkheads held firm. Gunners in the cruiser's stern turret spotted what they believed to be the attacking submarine and opened fire, but to no effect, though Lieutenant Commander Edward Bickford, RN, subsequently reported being depth charged. *Nürnberg* was soon underway at a speed of 16kts and made for port accompanied by *Köln*.

Leipzig was only capable of 12kts and Lütjens requested immediate support as British aircraft had begun harassing attacks, though they were successfully deterred by anti-aircraft fire. Saalwächter ordered all available craft despatched, as three of the minelaying destroyers finally reached the scene and the procession limped home. Both *Friedrich Ihn* and *Erich Steinbrinck* had been forced to break away directly to Wilhelmshaven with engine and fuel contamination problems. The seriously damaged *Leipzig* was under escort by two destroyers as well as the short-lived escort ships F7 and F9, minesweepers and R-boats when they were sighted by submarine HMS *Ursula* near the Elbe estuary the following day.

At 1115hrs, *Ursula* had penetrated the protective screen and fired four torpedoes at only 1,200yds distance. Two tremendous explosions were heard, the second buffeting *Ursula* so badly that several lights were blown out; however, *Ursula* withdrew, skilfully avoiding the German ships hunting it. The torpedoes had missed *Leipzig* and instead hit F9, which sank almost immediately with 120 men killed including *Geleitflottille* commander *Fregattenkapitän* Friedrich-Wilhelm Pindter. Only 34 survivors were rescued by *Räumboote*. The loss of F9 would be the sole casualty from this original *Geleitflottille*, the ships withdrawn from front-line service and the flotilla finally disbanded during May.

The successful destruction of 12 ships by the destroyers' minefield was insufficient recompense for the damage inflicted by the two British submarines. While *Nürnberg* was ready to sail once more in April 1940, *Leipzig* would never return to proper active service, relegated to a training role within the Baltic Sea. Neither were available to take part in the Norwegian invasion.

In Berlin, the effect of the submarine attacks was sobering. In its War Diary, SKL described German ASW work as 'either inadequate or non-existent', which further indicated battleship operations should only be undertaken in the northern portion of the North Sea. They noted that not a single enemy submarine had yet been confirmed destroyed. Berlin ordered more efficient

LEIPZIG HIT BY A TORPEDO FIRED BY HMS *SALMON* (overleaf)

On 13 December 1939 *Konteradmiral* Günther Lütjens was sailing in a zig-zagging holding pattern aboard his flagship *Nürnberg* in company with *Leipzig* and *Köln* on the eastern fringe of the North Sea. Lütjens had recently been appointed Commander in Chief Reconnaissance Forces (*Befehlshaber der Aufklärungsstreitkräfte*) and his three light cruisers had been tasked to rendezvous with destroyers returning from minelaying near Newcastle.

The idea of large ships escorting smaller ones appears counter intuitive as it is a reversal of their tried and tested traditional roles. That morning, British submarine HMS *Salmon* rammed the point home by torpedoing and damaging both *Leipzig* and *Nürnberg*, the former most severely. *Leipzig* was first to be hit, amidships below the waterline. Though *Leipzig* would limp home to Germany, it was never fully operational again.

planning and execution of ASW operations by *U-Jäger* combined with the use of greater numbers of depth charges and more persistence in attack like that shown by the Royal Navy. An increase in the use of ASW aircraft was also strongly advised, though inter-service rivalry – a bane of all Hitler's military services – between the Luftwaffe and Kriegsmarine would always hamper this.

Not until 7 January 1940 was a British submarine destroyed by direct German action; HMS *Undine* scuttled after attempting to torpedo auxiliary minesweeper *M1204 Anne Busse* travelling in company with *M1203 Bürgermeister Smidt I* 20 miles west of Heligoland. The single torpedo track was sighted and both minesweepers immediately commenced depth charge attacks that caused severe damage, forcing *Undine* to surface and be scuttled. Unfortunately, due to flooding, the submarine's scuttling charges were inaccessible, and though vent valves were opened the forward main vent remained shut, probably damaged by the depth charging. *Undine* retained enough buoyancy to allow Germans to board briefly, salvaging some unburnt confidential papers, before chlorine gas forced them out. Efforts to tow the submarine were abandoned as *Undine* sank upright in only 37m of water, later inspected by Kriegsmarine divers.

1940

The winter of 1939–40 turned out to be one of the worst for decades and operations were hampered for all belligerents in Northern Europe. Despite the atrocious winter conditions, further destroyer minelaying missions were completed during January and February. Royal Air Force patrols had been stepped up over the North Sea coastal region and Hudson bombers of 224 Squadron located and attacked retreating destroyers of 4th Destroyer Flotilla on the afternoon of 11 January near Horn Reef, ten miles off the westernmost point of Denmark. Intense flak from three destroyers foiled every approach and a Hudson piloted by Pilot Officer Richard Crozier Lloyd, RAF, was shot down, crashing into the sea killing all four crewmen.

In Sengwarden, MGK West was under pressure to utilize battleships *Scharnhorst* and *Gneisenau*. A single sortie in November against the British Northern Patrol that guarded the Faroes passage into the North Atlantic had resulted in the sinking of auxiliary cruiser HMS *Rawalpindi*, but *Flottenchef* Marschall had faced criticism for withdrawing at the first sighting of another approaching warship, though he was only strictly obeying standing orders not to take 'unnecessary risks'.

A new mission was planned during January, and directives for it were issued by SKL on the 23rd. As Saalwächter considered the condition of battleships

Dropping depth charges from a *U-Boot Jäger*. British submarines had acted with apparent impunity against Kriegsmarine forces during the early stages of the war. German ASW techniques and equipment were relatively undeveloped and protracted searches for likely contacts extremely rare. Not until January 1940 did the Kriegsmarine sink their first British submarine when HMS *Undine* was forced to surface and scuttle after being depth charged. (National Digital Archive, Poland)

Scharnhorst and *Gneisenau* unsuitable for Atlantic operations, a North Sea foray was ordered by Berlin. Operation *Nordmark* was designed to attack British ON (outbound from Britain) and HN (homebound) convoy traffic that travelled the route between the Shetland Islands and Bergen, Norway. The two battleships with heavy cruiser *Admiral Hipper* departed Wilhelmshaven under destroyer and torpedo boat escort on 18 February. However, within two days, *Nordmark* had completely failed. Destroyer *Z9 Wolfgang Zenker* was forced to turn back with ice damage, and all bar two of the remaining destroyers detached to undertake planned operations against merchant ships in the eastern Skagerrak. A lack of sighted ships led Marschall to deduce (correctly) that he had been detected, so the mission was aborted and all ships were returned to Wilhelmshaven. Marschall had been operating with limited direction and bitter recriminations followed, notably of MGK West. In Berlin, SKL believed that Saalwächter's office 'should not confine itself merely to sending the Commanding Admiral at sea incoming intelligence on the enemy situation … but should intervene in an operation actually in progress and issue clear directives, unmistakably defining the viewpoint of the command posts ashore who are the best informed as to the enemy situation'.[6]

Meanwhile, as the rumbling echoes of *Nordmark* died away, Luftwaffe reconnaissance reported the frequent presence of numerous unidentified fishing vessels near the Dogger Bank, strongly suspected to be enemy trawlers signalling about German shipping and aerial movements. Saalwächter ordered a destroyer attack, codenamed *Wikinger*.

At midday on 22 February *Fregattenkapitän* Fritz von Berger, aboard *Z16 Friedrich Eckoldt*, led *Z4 Richard Beitzen*, *Z13 Erich Koellner*, *Z6 Theodor Riedel*, *Z3 Max Schultz* and *Z1 Leberecht Maass* from Wilhelmshaven, carrying additional boarding parties for searching and possible seizure of suspect vessels. In the most disastrous consequence of inefficient communication between the Kriegsmarine and Luftwaffe, an He 111 bomber of KG 26 engaged on a mission to attack targets of opportunity between the Orkney Islands and Thames estuary misidentified the destroyers as they passed in line ahead formation north-west along the six-mile wide mine-free passage '*Weg* I' in the defensive Westwall minefield.

With neither ships nor aircraft issuing recognition signals, and after a number of passes overhead, the aircraft received several 20mm warning shots, returning machine gun fire and starting the first of two bomb runs. *Leberecht Maass* was hit between the forward superstructure and funnel on the first run and as *Friedrich Eckoldt* slowly approached to assess the damage and render aid, the second bomb run hit the damaged destroyer twice more. Beneath a huge fireball, *Leberecht Maass* broke in two and sank. To compound the confusion, *Max Schultz* then ran onto a mine recently laid in '*Weg* 1' by British destroyers HMS *Intrepid* and *Ivanhoe* two weeks previously. Believing a British submarine nearby, the other destroyers lowered boats for survivors while they departed to hunt the non-existent enemy. *Vorpostenboote* called to search for survivors were

---

6   SKL War Diary, 20 February 1940.

unable to leave harbour in heavy fog and only 60 of *Leberecht Maass*' 330 crew members were rescued and none of the 308 men from *Max Schultz*.

Within the destroyer service, morale perceptibly sagged. An investigation into the *Wikinger* disaster attributed blame to a combination of inexperienced aviators and inefficient staff briefings between the Luftwaffe and Kriegsmarine. A furious Hitler even issued his own directive on the matter, in which he demanded 'flawless reciprocal briefing' of command elements on movements on land, sea and air within the same operational area, and also requested the tightening of recognition signal regulations.

As plans percolated for an assault on the Low Countries and France – codenamed *Fall Gelb* and first mentioned in the SKL War Diary on 9 December 1939 as Hitler pondered what form the invasion may take – the focus abruptly shifted to Norway. Fears of a British invasion of Norway had rapidly taken root, not entirely without justification. Deciding to seize the impetus of control over Scandinavia, on 1 March 1940, SKL recorded detailed instructions from Hitler on the method by which Norway was to be taken. The Kriegsmarine and Luftwaffe were to 'bear the brunt of the first operation' and the invasion, codenamed *Weserübung*, was confirmed; *Wesertag* was set for 9 April 1940.

Virtually every surface unit of the Kriegsmarine was involved in this complicated and ambitious combined arms operation, which will be told in detail in a

OPERATION *NORDMARK*

Operation *Nordmark* was an abortive attempt at attacking Allied convoy traffic in the North Sea during 17–25 Feb, 1940. German intelligence detected a convoy travelling northwards along Britain's east coast which then turned and traversed the route between the Shetland Islands and Bergen, Norway. 'HN' convoys travelled from Bergen to Britain, carrying predominantly wood, while 'ON' convoys travelled east from Britain, gathering at the Shetlands before transiting to Bergen. British ore-carrying steamers travelling from Norway tended to head directly from Narvik to the Shetland Islands without joining the Bergen convoys. Convoy ON12 comprised ten British, eight Norwegian, two Swedish, two Danish, one Panamanian and four Finnish vessels.

On the evening of 17 February, *Flottenchef* Marschall moved his ships out of Wilhelmshaven to the Wangerooge Channel to avoid complications from icing in harbour. This was reported by RAF aircraft and, with the intensification of Luftwaffe reconnaissance activity over the area of the North Sea between the Shetlands and Norwegian coast, the Admiralty deduced the impending German operation.

Attempted RAF bombing of Marschall's ships was thwarted by fog and Marschall sailed on 18 February ready for battle. However, London had taken the decision to hold ON12 at Kirkwall until HMS *Rodney*, *Hood* and *Warspite* were available to provide cover.

In Berlin, SKL was reluctant to interfere with a battleship operation in progress, but considered the chance to encounter enemy traffic without heavy cover good. They expected Marschall to wait in the location he had reached north-east of the Shetlands, also expecting firm direction to be provided by MGK West. Instead Saalwächter's office issued intelligence updates with no conclusions. Unable to locate any enemy shipping even by use of floatplane aircraft, Marschall obeyed the mantra of 'no unnecessary risks' and retreated to Wilhelmshaven. Though he later faced recriminations for a perceived premature retreat, and Saalwächter more so for his lack of operational guidance, if the Royal Navy's heavy covering force had indeed encountered Marschall, he would still have been obliged to withdraw given the standing orders to avoid engaging heavy enemy units.

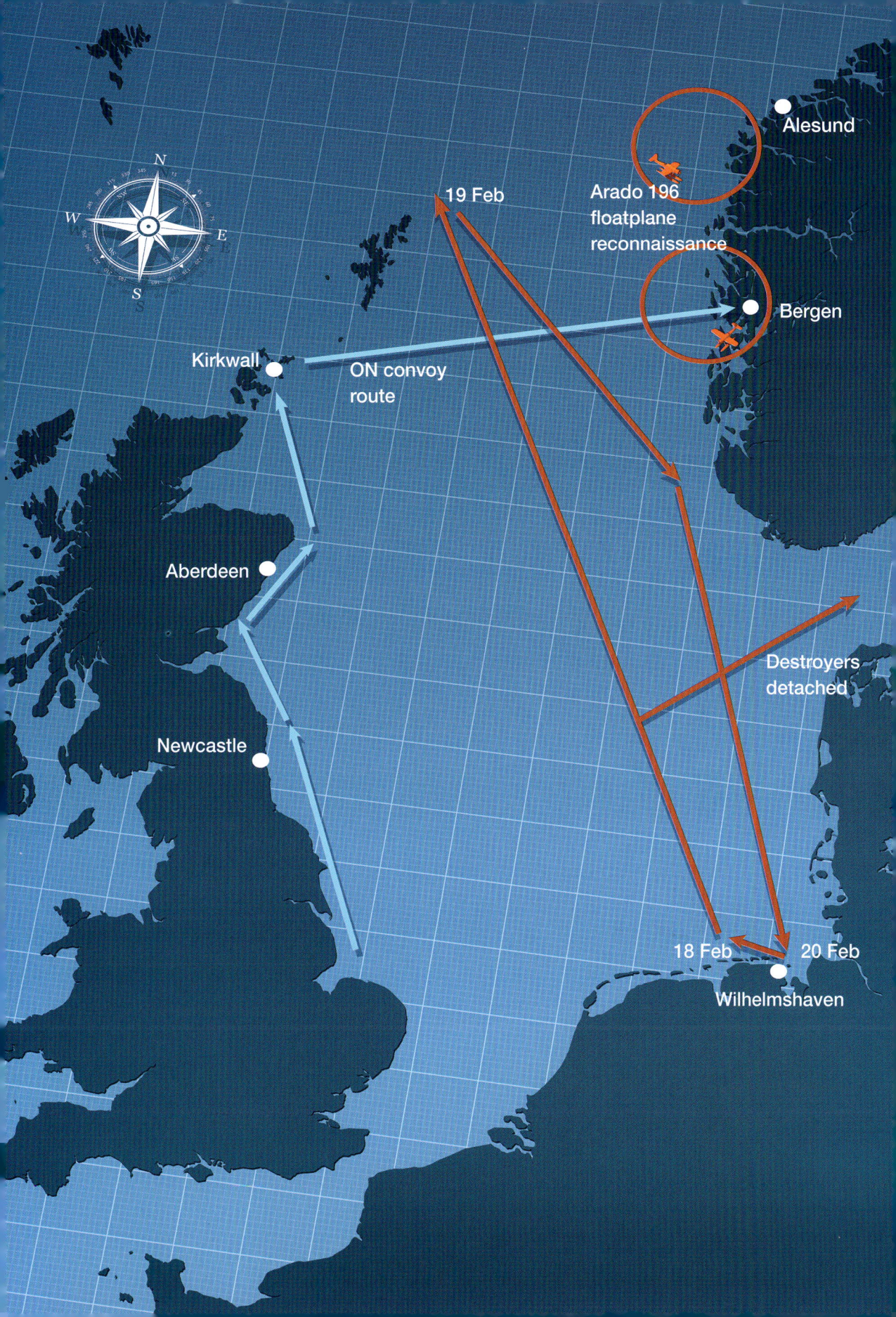

forthcoming volume. Of the complete destroyer force of 20, 16 took part with the remaining four only excluded as they were refitting in shipyards. The ultimate result of *Weserübung* was the successful German occupation of Denmark and Norway, but at such a severe cost that the Kriegsmarine was temporarily crippled.

By the end of *Weserübung* – with the final surrender of Norwegian troops on 10 June – the Kriegsmarine surface fleet had lost heavy cruiser *Blücher*, light cruisers *Karlsruhe* and *Königsberg*, three torpedo boats and 10 destroyers destroyed, as well as several minesweepers and assorted vessels of the security flotillas. Others were damaged to different degrees of severity and the loss of so many smaller ships contributed to a severe shortage of minesweepers and patrol vessels with which to fight what soon became a coastal naval war stretching far beyond German territorial waters. Of the destroyer force, only three remained operational, the others were all in dockyards except for *Z6 Theodor Riedel*, which had run aground and been beached in Norway for interim repairs to the hull. It would not sail to Germany until late June. All four existing destroyer flotillas were disbanded and survivors reassigned to the newly established 5th and 6th Destroyer Flotillas, though the golden time for German destroyers was now over.

While fighting had raged in Norway, the long-awaited invasion of the Low Countries and France – *Fall Gelb* – began on 10 May and was accomplished with a speed that surprised even the Germans. Luxembourg was subdued in one day and within four days The Netherlands had surrendered, Belgium following suit two weeks later. Outmanoeuvred from the outset, the British Expeditionary Force was pushed back to the English Channel and, after German armoured forces reached the coast on 20 May, began evacuating from Dunkirk and its environs in Operation *Dynamo*, which officially commenced seven days later.

A pre-war photograph showing men of the 1st S-Flotilla reloading their boat's starboard torpedo tube. (Fox Photos / Stringer)

With local sea conditions unsuitable for large vessels and U-boats, the sole Kriegsmarine threat to the evacuation was posed by S-boats; nine already relocated to the German Frisian island of Borkum to support *Fall Gelb*. An inaugural S-boat patrol to the north-east of the Dover Strait on the night of 9 May ended with a clash between three British destroyers that were converging in a spoiling attack on German minelayers and S31, which had been alerted to their presence by a Luftwaffe flying boat. S31 fired both torpedoes, one hitting HMS *Kelly* in the forward boiler room, ripping a 50-foot hole from keel to waterline. The ship immediately stopped, swiftly developing a 13° list to starboard. Unsure of whether the attacker was a U-boat, accompanying HMS *Bulldog* was ordered to drop depth charges as the S-boat retreated. In thickening fog *Bulldog* took the stricken *Kelly* in tow and, at a little past midnight, high-speed engines were heard. Minutes later S33 appeared out of the fog, accidentally ramming into HMS *Bulldog*'s starboard quarter at an oblique angle. The S-boat was deflected forward into HMS *Kelly* as the German crew began firing both the forward machine gun and stern-mounted flak weapon, striking *Kelly* at the break of the forecastle. With the listing destroyer's starboard deck awash, S33 drove at high speed along the deck, tearing loose the ship's whaler and motor cutter as well as smashing davits and guardrails. Aboard S33 there was pandemonium as the steel guardrail stanchions tore through the wooden hull, smashing the bow to pieces. In moments S33 broke away, disappearing into the fog, the engines stuttering and dying as the helmsman had fallen across the throttle lever after the collision, cutting the throttle completely. Neither side was visible to each other; *Bulldog* and *Kelly* continuing their slow limp to shipyards on the River Tyne as S33 did likewise to Wilhelmshaven, where it was immediately consigned to the shipyard.

S-boat missions into the Channel reconnoitred Ostend, Nieuport and Dunkirk and on 21 May S32 sank a darkened steamer near Nieuport, the huge explosion and sheets of flame prompting the captain to report it as 'probably carrying fuel or munitions'. Presumed sunk, this could have been minesweeper HMS *Corburn* lost that night to unconfirmed causes.

Of more certainty was the sinking of French destroyer *Jaguar*, one of three French destroyers carrying explosives and demolition crews from Brest to prepare Channel ports for destruction. Alerted by accurate B-Dienst radio intelligence, S21 and S23 lay in wait and at approximately 0045hrs they fired all torpedoes, one from Christiansen's S23 hitting *Jaguar* on the port side immediately below the bridge. The burning ship was towed towards shore and abandoned near the beach of Malo-les-Bains with 13 men killed in the attack and 23 injured.

S-boats were incrementally moved closer to the front line, all available craft putting into newly conquered Den Helder on 23 May after which nightly torpedo patrols were mounted against naval forces near Dunkirk. The situation had become increasingly chaotic for the Allies. On 27 May Operation *Dynamo*

S30 TORPEDOES HMS *WAKEFUL* (overleaf)

Fortunately for the Allied evacuation of Dunkirk, the Kriegsmarine were still reeling from severe losses suffered in Norway. Only S-boats and a handful of small Type II coastal U-boats were able to interfere with evacuation shipping. However, casualties were still inflicted by the Kriegsmarine; the loss of HMS *Wakeful* was one of the biggest disasters to befall *Dynamo* shipping. Oberleutnant zur See Wilhelm Zimmermann's S30 had sailed from Den Helder to operate near the well-lit Kwinte Buoy alongside S25 and S34. Zimmermann was waiting near the buoy when *Wakeful* was seen approaching. The destroyer carried about 640 troops onboard, all having been ordered below decks to areas as low as possible to maintain ship stability. They were stuffed into the engine room, boiler rooms and storerooms and as the destroyer neared Kwinte Buoy to begin a westward turn, Zimmermann's two torpedo tracks were seen; one avoided, the other struck the forward boiler room. *Wakeful* was cut in two and the halves sank immediately until the ends grounded in the sand bank. Only 47 crew and ten soldiers were later rescued; nine of the soldiers were later killed when their rescue ship HMS *Grafton* was subsequently torpedoed by U62.

began and the following day Belgium formally surrendered. For their part, the German High Command then committed a major blunder when land forces that had the Allies pinned inside the Dunkirk pocket were ordered to halt before a final attack. Göring's Luftwaffe was to be used to pound the British into submission, a task they were ultimately unable to complete.

S-boats were exhorted to intensify pressure on *Dynamo* shipping, though the RAF had recognized the threat and established 'anti-E-boat sweeps' as the British evacuation got underway. Nonetheless, the 694-ton steamer *Abukir* crowded with more than 200 British troops was sunk by S34 on 28 May. Mistakenly believing they were under attack by U-boat, soldiers aboard the ship opened fire with a Lewis Gun at what they thought to be a surfaced conning tower, instead hitting crowded lifeboats. The following night three S-boats sailed from Den Helder to operate near the well-lit Kwinte Buoy. Using the *Lauertaktik* principle – in which S-boats were spaced one nautical mile apart, approaching the presumed target convoy in line before dividing on a broad front and attacking – two mounted an unsuccessful attack on sloop HMS *Shearwater* south of Fairy Bank. Meanwhile, S30 sighted a destroyer approaching, leading a straggling column of ships.

HMS *Wakeful* had taken 640 troops off the Dunkirk beach, all housed below decks to lessen topweight on the destroyer. Of two torpedoes fired from S30 at a 600m range, one narrowly missed the bow, but the second hit amidships on the starboard beam. *Wakeful* was split clean in two by the explosion and sank in seconds. Three officers, one Petty Officer, the ship's surgeon, one NAAFI worker, 92 naval ratings and all but ten of the embarked soldiers were killed in either the explosion or rapid sinking, trapped below decks before they had any chance to escape. The S-boat retreated to reload as British ships arrived to rescue whatever survivors they could find. Unfortunately for them, their numerous signal lights and flares attracted the small Type II coastal U-boat U62 which torpedoed destroyer HMS *Grafton*. In the pandemonium that followed, both S30 and U62 faded into the darkness while frantically manoeuvring British ships collided and nervously opened fire at one another.

The S-boats' success at fast moving hit and run operations proved the exceptional abilities of the boats and their highly motivated crews, and on 30 May SKL ordered all operational S-boats immediately placed under the direct control of MGK West to maximize their effectiveness. The advantage was squarely in the hands of the Kriegsmarine, though they lacked the numbers to fully capitalize on it.

On 30 May S24 torpedoed the French destroyer *Cyclone* near Kwinte Bank. Flagship of France's 2nd Destroyer Flotilla, *Cyclone* was

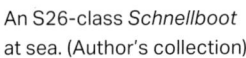
An S26-class *Schnellboot* at sea. (Author's collection)

heading to Dunkirk when a torpedo hit the bow; it was damaged so severely that the S-boat crew claimed it sunk. However, despite the bow section having been completely blasted away, *Cyclone* was afloat and capable of maintaining a speed of 5kts, escorted slowly by Polish destroyer *Blyskawica* to Dover.

Nearby and less than ten minutes later, another French destroyer, *Sirocco*, passed in front of the stationary S23 and S26 and was hit by two torpedoes, one from each boat. The first double salvo had grazed the destroyer's bow without exploding, the second pair hit the stern. *Sirocco* was laden with 770 troops plucked from the beaches of Dunkirk; nearby destroyer HMS *Vega* reporting a column of flame nearly 200ft high that illuminated the end of the French ship. Immobilized and listing badly to starboard she went down in two minutes with 59 crew and over 600 troops aboard as well as the colours of the 92nd French Infantry Regiment, which its colonel had risked his life to smuggle out of Lille after encirclement by German troops.

Marinegruppenkommando West ambitiously planned to move 1st S-Flotilla to a forward base at Boulogne-sur-Mer where it was felt that, in conjunction with torpedo boats and hastily established heavy shore batteries at Calais, it could contribute to the complete blocking of the English Channel. However, at sea, S-boats had begun to encounter greater obstacles than ever with repeated air attacks, thick fog and enemy ships firing flares into the night sky that prevented any approach to Dunkirk. As *Dynamo* reached its climax it was apparent that the Allies had temporarily neutralized the S-boat threat despite MGK West throwing every available boat into the fray.

The focus switched from Dunkirk to Channel and east coast convoy traffic, now within comfortable range for S-boats operating from captured harbours. *Dynamo* officially ended on 4 June 1940 and on 22 June, France signed an armistice that came into force three days later. With increased Luftwaffe cover from captured French airfields, *Schnellboote* began planning torpedo and mine-laying missions though the latter were prohibited along the southern English coast. The Luftwaffe had requested mines within 25 miles of the shoreline to force convoys further out to sea and to make them more vulnerable to air attack, but SKL forbade this as it could interfere with any prospective invasion landings. Not until 2 August did it relent and allow minelaying off Portsmouth and Southampton.

German intelligence reported increased numbers of Royal Navy MTBs being deployed between Dover and Ramsgate to counter the S-boats. Lively merchant

The 38cm guns of the Siegfried naval battery, built near the hamlet of Audinghen, Pas de Calais. The woods of Haringzelles in which the battery was located were planted by German troops to help camouflage the emplacement. This photograph shows construction on the concrete bunkers in which the guns would finally be sheltered; the casemates were completed by the end of 1941. (Interfoto / Alamy Stock Photo)

traffic was also detected running along the south coast of England, so SKL surmised that if the British accepted the increased risk of this sea route closest to German forces, then the Thames remained a main supply hub. SKL deduced that British west coast ports were probably struggling to handle the volume of convoyed supplies that required onwards shipping; the route trailing around the north of Britain and down the east coast constituted a significant detour that would consume valuable fuel and time while still making ships vulnerable to mines, aircraft and S-boats. Expecting heavy Channel convoys, Boulogne and Cherbourg became the major French S-boat harbours, so that the entire British south coast was exposed to attack.

On 20 July, SKL recorded convoys of between 14 and 17 ships sighted close to the British coast, and stressed the need for the speedy expansion of strong coastal batteries in the Cape Gris Nez area and relentless Luftwaffe operations. Though hazardous in the extreme, CW (westbound) and CE (eastbound) Channel convoys had been established between the Bristol Channel and the Thames. Large merchant ships were prohibited by the British Admiralty to sail in these convoys as S-boats and aircraft exacted a steady toll despite Royal Navy MTB and destroyer opposition. On 25 July, CW8 was so badly mauled that the Admiralty suspended Channel convoys, resumed in early August. On the other side, despite objections from the F.d.T., S-boats were also tasked with minelaying to close the Thames to merchant traffic. Bütow's main concern was that the use of fast attack craft in this role was contrary to every principle of successful S-boat operations, and they were also only capable of carrying a small number of mines each. Nonetheless, he was overruled and minelaying became as commonplace as torpedo patrols.

In the skies above, the battle between the Luftwaffe and Royal Air Force raged as each struggled for aerial domination over southern England and the Channel. Between occupied Rotterdam and Le Havre a huge potential invasion force of transports, barges, lighters, tugboats and motorboats of various types and sizes had been gathered in preparation for an invasion of Britain. Wehrmacht and Waffen SS troops rehearsed disembarkation from crudely adapted landing craft and in Britain invasion fever reached epidemic levels. Air attacks mounted by the Luftwaffe on the night of 7 September (the first night of 'The Blitz') were so intense that the code word signifying invasion imminent – 'Cromwell' – was issued in south-east England; church bells were rung and the army and Home Guard mobilized. To counter the threat, Royal Air Force Bomber Command began night bombing raids that sank nearly 200 barges by mid-September while the Royal Navy also mounted spoiling attacks with MGBs and destroyers, sinking German trawlers near the Channel ports and bombarding harbours such as Cherbourg and Le Havre. In reality, the Kriegsmarine was aghast at the idea of an amphibious invasion attempt as it was woefully under-equipped and still reeling from the extreme losses inflicted in Norway. Raeder presented Hitler with a stark warning that the levels of commitment to *Seelöwe* could be maintained only until mid-October without jeopardizing other theatres of action, and finally a Führer conference on 14 September resulted in its indefinite postponement. Although Hitler was unwilling to cancel absolutely lest the enemy's morale received an unwelcome boost, the massed invasion shipping was dispersed. Finally, on 12 October, the Führer decided that until spring 'preparations for *Seelöwe* shall be continued solely for the purpose of maintaining political and military pressure on England'. The Battle of Britain was over and the Luftwaffe had failed to gain the requisite air supremacy to accommodate any invasion attempt, which was ultimately abandoned. Hitler's attention had already switched to the Soviet Union.

A German sailor on the beach at Le Havre. The fall of The Netherlands, Belgium and France enabled the occupation of harbours stretching the entire length of Britain's southern coast with its potentially vulnerable convoy traffic. (United Archives GmbH / Alamy Stock Photo)

With *Seelöwe* indefinitely postponed, the Kriegsmarine returned to the disruption of Britain's maritime supply and communication lines and the preservation of German ones. Aerial mining of ports and shipping lanes became more prolific. While destroyers that had been moved to occupied Brest laid fields in the west of the English Channel, the central Channel was handled by torpedo boats and the south-east by S-boats. *Marinegruppenkommando* West held responsibility for these actions, its operational boundary line with MGK North stretching from Cromer to Den Helder, which caused jurisdictional problems.

Generaladmiral Carls' MGK North strongly urged the relocation of a flotilla of S-boats to its area of control and a 'tug of war' between Saalwächter and him ensued, while F.d.T. Bütow firmly resisted any division of strength from his south-east English coast focal point. The S-boats' presence had become so prominent there that the convoy passage between Lowestoft and Great Yarmouth became known in Britain as 'E-boat Alley'. Torpedo boats which had been minelaying in the Dover Strait since August lacked the shallow draught required to approach as close inshore as S-boats, which could even pass unobstructed over some enemy minefields. Nonetheless, despite the boundary between MGK West and North being moved northwards from Cromer to Hull to remove confusion over Thames operations, Bütow was partially overruled and the 1st S-Flotilla transferred to MGK North for east coast operations.

Under Carls' control, on 6 November 1940 seven of his under-utilized torpedo boats attempted to attack two coastal convoys reported heading north just off the Scottish coast. However, they ran into a British minefield off Kinnaird's Head that sank T6; 48 men were lost and the remaining torpedo boats returned to port after their last major North Sea sortie.

The end of year balance sheet for the Kriegsmarine proved largely unsatisfactory. Surface torpedo attacks had sunk 28 ships in the last seven months of 1940 and Luftwaffe and Kriegsmarine minelaying had destroyed 201 ships during the entire year. As U-boats had discovered during the same period, mines were more effective than torpedoes, although minelaying was unpopular among crews; it was considered a dangerous and largely inconclusive task with results often unknown and achievements unsung.

1941

The first few months of the year yielded little success for the Kriegsmarine in either the Channel or coastal North Sea in the face of bad weather and strengthening British defences. By April, the first phase of concerted S-boat operations in these areas was over, and during May all three regional flotillas transferred from the English Channel and North Sea to support the impending attack on the Soviet Union, replaced by 4th S-Flotilla that had been formed in October 1940 and was composed of older boats. The Royal Air Force increased its strength along the Channel coast in 1941, hampering Luftwaffe reconnaissance; the resultant lack of convoy sightings impacted S-boat mission planning with sorties infrequent and results poor. The emphasis returned once again to minelaying, particularly between Portland and Portsmouth. Frequently under fire from coastal batteries, the S-boats suffered neither loss nor did they achieve any discernible results.

However, despite aggressive Royal Navy coastal forces, the English Channel remained a primary German conduit for surface ships to the Bay of Biscay, generally undertaken at night in short hops between guarded harbours. Between April and June 1941, 29 major ships and 11 destroyers passed through the English Channel unscathed. Disguised merchant raiders were also successfully routed that way towards the Atlantic, with *Schiff 28 Michel* making the voyage during March, escorted by five torpedo boats, nine R-boats and eight minesweepers. Aware of the German movements, the Royal Navy planned an interception, but careless radio chatter gave their approach away and attacks by MTB, MGB and destroyer attacks were repulsed with ferocious gunfire while being illuminated by star shells from German coastal batteries.

S-boats of the 6th S-Flotilla that was formed in 1941 and immediately used for North Sea and English Channel missions. These boats carry the 'skull cap' (*Kalotte*); an armoured bridge enclosure that was fitted as standard from late 1942 onwards. (National Digital Archive, Poland)

While the single flotilla of tired old S-boats achieved the near impossible of keeping an offensive presence within English waters, the Royal Navy and Royal Air Force had been granted breathing space to rearm and reorganize coastal and anti-shipping strike forces. With invasion fears receded, forces that had been held in reserve were now available for front line duty.

The combat pattern of S-boats attempting to find British coastal convoys, exploit gaps in ever more effective defensive screens and launch attacks remained near constant for the months that followed. But their effectiveness was dimming. During October 1941, the RAF used radar-guided aircraft for the first time in convoy defence, with six Beaufort torpedo bombers dedicated to the task. The number of German-speaking 'headache' radio intelligence operators aboard Royal Navy ships at sea was dramatically increased to take advantage of the S-boats' Achilles heel, their reliance on clear language VHF transmissions to coordinate torpedo attacks.

Not until November was the overstretched 4th S-Flotilla reinforced once more by the 1st S-Flotilla returning from the Baltic fight against the Russians. Others were posted to the Mediterranean Sea as Germany's war had expanded to more fronts than the Kriegsmarine could support.

Taken from an escorting Royal Navy ship, Kriegsmarine shore battery shells fall around a British Channel convoy, 5 November 1940. The major Kriegsmarine batteries on the Pas de Calais posed a significant threat to Channel shipping. (Superstock / Alamy Stock Photo)

1942

Hamstrung once more over the winter months by bad weather conditions, *Kapitänleutnant* Niels Bätge's 4th S-Flotilla was diverted to an audacious Kriegsmarine plan during February, his boats providing flank coverage for Operation *Cerberus* – the spectacularly successful dash through the English Channel by capital ships *Scharnhorst*, *Gneisenau* and *Prinz Eugen*.

Alternating torpedo and minelaying missions resumed almost as soon as *Cerberus* was completed. The coastal route from Dover to Dungeness and the North Sea convoy track within the Smith's Knoll–Ordfordness area were targeted using timer-equipped mines for the first time.

Within the English Channel, British coastal forces stepped up offensive action in the first months of the year and S-boats were more frequently ambushed along operational approach and return routes, requiring their own covering forces. A proposal to provide torpedo boats was turned down by MGK West, which judged them vulnerable to mines and outgunned by British destroyers. Instead, *Räumboote* were considered, the newer models bristling with flak weapons. Although there were already too few available to escort German convoys trailing towards western France, hard-pressed R-boats were chosen to rendezvous with returning S-boats and provide flak coverage, either kept at immediate readiness in harbour or on station along the S-boats' planned routes.

The overall effectiveness of minelaying was also called into question during February and March as naval intelligence determined that British radar stations were accurately plotting minefield locations, not only allowing them to be effectively swept, but also re-routing convoy traffic to clearer waters.

Räumboote of the 4th *Räumboote* Flotilla. This flotilla, under the command of *Korvettenkapitän* Waldemar Holst, was formed in April 1940 for North Sea service. Following the occupation of France, they relocated to Boulogne-sur-Mer. (Author's collection)

Correspondingly, the F.d.T. suspended further minelaying until the issue could be addressed. However, MGK West disagreed with his judgement, reasoning that even if minefields were detected, merchant traffic was still forced wide of the coast and vulnerable to torpedo attack. Although operations by S-boats were severely limited due to bad weather, the sowing of mines was resumed on 3 April by both flotillas that sailed with combined torpedo and mine loads.

Along the conquered European coastline massive German resources were expended on the creation of the Atlantic Wall, particularly concrete fortifications around major ports and docks. Additionally, an intensive minelaying schedule created an east–west barrier between Boulogne and Cherbourg to protect coastal convoys. Minelayers, destroyers, torpedo boats, minesweepers and *Räumboote* were all utilized, frequently bringing them into contact with British forces either attempting to disrupt the minelaying or in the process of dropping their own offensive barrages.

During August, German intelligence reported an unexpected increase of radio traffic and landing craft numbers in England's southern port. Fears of an attempted Allied landing on the French coast grew until it materialized on the morning of 19 August with Anglo-Canadian forces landing at Dieppe in Operation *Jubilee*. Unfortunately for the *Jubilee* forces, German coastal troops were already on alert.

During the early morning hours, a small German convoy, consisting of five coasters under escort by *UJ1411 Treff III*, *UJ1404 Franken* and minesweeper *M4015*, had blundered into British Naval Group 5 headed for Dieppe, a procession of craft carrying 325 men of 3 Commando, 40 US Army Rangers, five Free Frenchmen and an officer, and three men from the 'Phantom' signals unit. Despite unidentified hydrophone and radar traces having been detected by both sides, no attempt was made to divert from either course and they clashed fiercely resulting in the Royal Navy *SGB5* (Steam Gun Boat 5, renamed HMS *Grey Owl* in 1943) being severely damaged with 40 per cent of the crew wounded and *U-boot Jäger UJ1404* ablaze and sinking; the remaining ships, both German and Allied, scattered after the brief battle.

Though MGK West initially believed the engagement was probably the result of a routine MTB attack, shore defences were alerted. At 0535hrs three small patrol vessels of Dieppe's *Hafenschutzflottille* (Harbour Defence Flotilla) were also attacked just offshore and a prearranged flare signal fired that alerted the entire coastal region and brought Wehrmacht troops into action.

The Allied landing was a disaster. Of 6,106 men that had departed England, 1,027 were dead by the end of the day and 2,240 captured. The order for withdrawal had been given at 0950hrs following pitched battles against well-motivated Wehrmacht troops and under intense pressure from the Luftwaffe that fielded its new Fw190 fighters, outclassing the covering Royal Air Force, which lost 106 aircraft to the Germans' 48.

The remnants of a German convoy that had started the battle sailed for Le Treport, though the 159-ton armed tanker *Franz* had attempted to add firepower from its 88mm cannon by sailing towards Dieppe's beach and firing upon landing craft and Canadian troops. In return it was hit by naval gunfire and driven ashore in flames. S-boats played no part in the Dieppe battle, engaged elsewhere on minelaying and torpedo patrols.

Though Operation *Jubilee* could hardly be described as successful, it had two important results. Firstly, it helped convince OKW to fortify ports that they felt (incorrectly) would be a focal point of any Allied invasion. Secondly, it showed to the Allies the folly of just such an attack, leading to the design and construction of mobile Mulberry supply harbours that could be employed along any suitable stretch of coastline, such as the sweeping beaches of Normandy.

As winter approached so too did bad weather; several S-boats were forced to abort missions with engine damage caused by the heightened strain such conditions put on the boats. To the east, high winds prevented much activity from the three flotillas stationed in The Netherlands until 12 December when reliable Luftwaffe reports led a combined force of 17 S-boats to convoy FN89. Proving Admiralty fears regarding poor station keeping correct, this convoy of 38 merchants straggled over five miles presenting an almost impossible protection task for its escorts. Five merchants were sunk, in return S105 took damage from shellfire but suffered no casualties. Though considered a triumph, such successes for the S-boats were becoming noticeably few. Almost imperceptibly at first, the Kriegsmarine's stance was changing from offensive to defensive and impetus for the coastal battle in the North Sea and English Channel was passing to the British. Though there would be sporadic local German successes until the last months of the war, the coastal offensive had failed.

ANALYSIS

Germany's coastal campaign that began in the North Sea before expanding to the English Channel initially looked set to cause extreme hardship for Britain. The crucial supply of coal from the northern coalfields to the south-east proved

By the end 1942, the Kriegsmarine was vastly overstretched and the coastal war in the North Sea and English Channel had been fought and lost. Despite sporadic victories, over the following years nothing would alter the steady decline of the German Navy. (Mauritius Images GmbH / Alamy Stock Photo)

vulnerable to attack and smaller fleet units such as destroyers and S-boats rose to the challenge. However, even when the assault was not blunted by faulty torpedo weaponry or imperfect powerplants, it was always mounted by ships too few in number to ever prove decisive. Minelaying was periodically successful with ports and channels briefly closed and traffic diverted, but not to a degree that seriously affected industry or power supply in the vulnerable south-east of England.

Several repetitive threads weakened the military tapestry of the Third Reich and this coastal campaign is no exception. First, the battle was fought by a woefully under-strength navy. The dictates of the Versailles Treaty had successfully emasculated the German military as had been intended. Despite the somewhat ingenious methods of covert military development being undertaken during the inter-war period, the very nature of keeping it hidden meant it was always going to be a slower developmental process than if undertaken in the public eye. The mythology that Germany entered the war with the most cutting-edge weapons on the European battlefield is demonstrably false. Though possessing some superb, specialized weapons, German designs ranging from tanks to aircraft were frequently no match for their opponents' equivalent. The true genesis of German military success in the early years was in the high level of training received by aggressively talented soldiers, sailors and airmen, rather than much of the equipment with which they fought. That strong cadre of men trained during peacetime would have soon dwindled as casualty lists grew.

Second, Germany lacked a clear strategic arc in which to follow its war aims. At no point was a decisive strategy implemented, but rather measures were taken that were frequently *reactive* to events rather than proactively shaping the course of action. This is demonstrated by the sheer fact that Raeder had not even expected war with Britain – the nation possessing the most powerful and experienced European navy – until virtually the last moment. That he blindly believed Hitler's assurances is its own issue that could be argued as being naïve at best; nevertheless, he and the Kriegsmarine were unprepared for such an undertaking. Also, the fact that Hitler expected peace overtures to Britain to reap dividends as late as mid-1940 displayed not only his misjudgement of the enemy, but the lack of any sound strategic planning to defeat or at least neutralize this island nation.

Third, the kind of inter-service rivalry that permeated throughout the entire Wehrmacht robbed the Navy of powerful opportunities. Most damning of all was Göring's insistence of dominance over all military aircraft. This petty preoccupation with control robbed the Kriegsmarine of the potential presented by a dedicated naval air arm that could have exerted greater influence over German coastal warfare.

The high-tide point for the Wehrmacht was arguably just after the fall of France when Germany had successfully occupied swathes of Scandinavia and western Europe. The idea of invading Britain was clearly beyond the Wehrmacht's capability, but, if nothing else, Germany had bought time as British forces reeled from their defeat in France. Beyond that point, although experiencing instances of battlefield success, Germany's slim military power became vastly over-committed to theatres of action that eventually stretched from the waters off the American coast to the African sands and onwards to the steppes of the Soviet Union. An understrength Kriegsmarine acted in various capacities on all fronts; coastal forces involved in the North Sea and English Channel were frequently robbed of assets to bolster far-flung battlefields. German destroyers had already passed their most successful period with their minelaying sorties in British waters; never fully recovering from the severe losses in Norway and though reinforced with several ships of improved designs, they achieved little else of lasting value in any theatre. Neither did the frequently unsung crews of the torpedo boats. That is not to say that they did not achieve local combat successes; such as the sinking of HMS *Limbourne* and *Charybdis* in the English Channel during 1943.

Destroyers in action. (Author's collection)

The same could be said of the S-boats. By the end of 1942, despite also experiencing sporadic localized successes before the end of the war, these last truly effective offensive units within that region were engaged in a war of attrition they had no hope of winning. In total during 1942 they sank two destroyers, one motor launch, four trawlers and 19 merchant ships. They had captured an MGB, damaged three merchants with torpedoes, another two destroyers and one freighter was also damaged through mines, while the relentless minelaying destroyed five more freighters. However, compared with the sheer volume of coastal convoy traffic – 21,552 individual passages both north- and southbound along the east coast alone – the predation achieved by S-boats could be seen as almost insignificant. That, of course, does not diminish the bravery and sacrifice of sailors both merchant and military on both sides of the action at sea.

On the Allied side, while S-boats were being spread thinly throughout Germany's theatres of war, the British and Allied forces present in Britain had steadily built up their forces in opposition. Newer, larger and better-armed Fairmile D 'Dog Boats' were coming out of shipyards, a versatile design able to be fitted out as either MGB or MTB and a fearsome adversary. Inter-service Allied cooperation also reached new levels of efficiency, which the Kriegsmarine and Luftwaffe never matched.

The last of the Kriegsmarine's coastal forces – the security flotillas – was also stretched to crisis point by 1942. A critical lack of escort vessels for convoys carrying ore to Germany endangered the entire war economy, while the supply by maritime convoy of ammunition and equipment to occupied French ports was increasingly under threat. Indeed, on 30 April 1942, of 201 escort vessels stationed within the area controlled by MGK West, 115 were unserviceable through damage or essential maintenance; a predicament that had existed since 1940 when only a quarter of the auxiliary vessel numbers demanded by SKL had been raised from either newly constructed vessels or those captured. Insufficient manufacturing of steel, dockyard space and workers undermined construction or conversion of anywhere near enough craft.

Nonetheless, the coastal war would continue beyond 1942, though with German successes decreasing in regularity. Eventually, British coastal waters would receive fresh attention from U-boats in the last months of the war; an unexpected and briefly profitable offensive, though another military adventure doomed to ultimate failure.

FURTHER READING

Barnett, Correlli, *Engage the Enemy More Closely*, Hodder & Stoughton, London, 1992.

Bekker, Cajus, *Hitler's Naval War*, MacDonald & Jane's, London, 1974.

Bird, Keith W., 'The Origins and Role of German Naval History in the Interwar Period 1918–1939', *Naval War College Review*, Vol. 32, No. 2, Rhode Island, March–April 1979.

Bowyer, Chaz, *Men of Coastal Command 1939–1945,* William Kimber, London, 1985.

Chazette, Alain and Reberac, Fabian, *Kriegsmarine,* Éditions Heimdel, Bayeux, 1997.

Churchill, Winston, *The Second World War* (6 Vols), Cassell & Co., London, 1954.

Collier, Richard, *The Sands of Dunkirk*, Dutton, 1961.

Cooper, Bryan, *The E-Boat Threat*, MacDonald & Jane's, London, 1976.

Forty, George, *Fortress Europe,* Ian Allen Publishing, London, 2002.

German Underwater Ordnance, US Navy Bureau of Ordnance, Washington DC, 1946.

Haarr, Geirr, *The Gathering Storm: The Naval War in Northern Europe*, Seaforth Publishing, London, 2012.

Hümmelchen, Gerhard, *Die Deutschen Schnellboote*, E.S. Mittler & Sohn Verlag, Hamburg, 1996.

Isby, David, *The Luftwaffe and the War at Sea 1939–1945*, Chatham Publishing, London, 2005.

Lohmann W. and Hildebrand H.H., *Die Deutsche Kriegsmarine 1939–1945* (3 Vols), Podzun Verlag, Bad Nauheim, 1956.

Mallmann Showell, Jak P., *Führer Conferences on Naval Affairs*, Chatham Publishing, London, 2005.

Paterson, Lawrence, *Eagles over the Sea, Vol.1, 1935–1942,* Seaforth Publishing, London, 2019.

Paterson, Lawrence, *Hitler's Forgotten Flotillas*, Seaforth Publishing, London, 2017.

Paterson, Lawrence, *Schnellboote*, Seaforth Publishing, London, 2015.

Raeder, Erich, *Grand Admiral*, De Capo, 2001. First published USNI 1960 as *My Life*.

Rohwer, J. and Hümmelchen, G., *Chronik des Seekrieges 1939–1945*, Gerhar Stalling Verlag, 1968.

Stellmann, Georg, *Tagebuch und Briefe eines Minensuchers 1939–1946*, Books on Demand, Norderstedt, 2006.

Whitley, M.J., *Destroyer!*, Arms and Armour Press, London, 1983.

INDEX

Figures in **bold** refer to illustrations.

anti-submarine warfare (ASW) 18–21, 42, 52, 57, **60**
Atlantic Ocean 4–8, 11, 15, 34–35, 43–44, 47, 52, 60–61, 72

Baltic Sea 4, 14, 16, 26, 29, 38, 48, **56**, 57, 73
battleships 6–7, 11–12, 14, 52, 54–55, **56**, 57, 60–61, **62**
    Gneisenau 6, 11, 52–53, 60–61, 73
    Scharnhorst 6, 11, 14, 60–61, 73
Belgium 10, **31**, **35**, **37**, 38, 46, 64, 68, **71**
Berlin 17, 34, 42, 57, 61, **62**
Boulogne-sur-Mer (Boulogne) **21**, **36**, 39, 42, **45**, 46–47, 69–70, **74**
Britain 4–7, **8**, 10–12, **13**, 17–18, 26–27, 29, **31**, 35, **36**, 42–44, 48–49, 52, 61, **62**, 70, **71**, 75–77

Calais **8**, **9**, 10, **36**, **45**, 46, 69
Carls, *Generaladmiral* Rolf **37**, **38**, **43**, 71
Cherbourg **36**, 42, **45**, 46–47, 70, 74
Cromer **31**, **36**, 38, 55, 71
cruisers 6, 7, 11, **12**, **13**, 14, 17–18, 33, 40, **41**, **48**, **49**, 52, 54–55, **56**, **57**, 60–61, 64
    Admiral Hipper 6, 11, 40, 56, 61
    Köln 13, 48, 52, **56**, **57**
    Königsberg **13**, 48, **49**, 64
    Leipzig **6**, **7**, 13, 48, 56, **57**
    Nürnberg 13, 48, 56, **57**

Den Helder **37**, 38, 46, **65**, 68, 71
Densch, *Vizeadmiral* Hermann 13, **37**, 40, **44**, 48
depth charges 14, 18, 20–21, 24, **25**, 30, 52, 57, **60**, 64
destroyers 6–7, 10–13, **14**, **15**, 16–20, **21**, 26, **27**, **28**, 30, **31**, 33, 35, 38, **39**, 40–41, 47–49, 52, **53**, **54**, **55**, **56**, **57**, 60–62, **63**, 64, **65**, 68–74, 76, **77**
    Z1 Leberecht Maass 6, 14, **15**, 61–62
    Z3 Max Schultz **31**, 52, 61–62
    Z14 Friedrich Ihn **31**, 52, 56–57
Dover **8**, **9**, 10, **31**, **36**, **45**, 49, 69, 73
Dunkirk **9**, **36**, 42, **45**, 64, **65**, 68–69

English Channel 4–5, 10–11, **21**, 30, 35, 42–43, **44**, 48–49, 64–65, 69–71, **72**, **73**, 75, **76**, 77

flak weapons 14, 17, 19–20, 24–25, **42**, 47, 60, 65, 73
Fleischer, *Konteradmiral* Wilhelm **37**, 39–40, 44
Flottenchef, Fleet Commander **16**, 35, 40, 49, 60, **62**
flotillas 6, **10**, 11, 15–17, **19**, **20**, **21**, **32**, 35, **37**, 38, 40–42, 46, 48, 52, 55, 57, 60, **64**, 68–69, 71, **72**, 73, **74**, 75, 78

France 4–5, 10, 12–13, **20**, **31**, **35**, **36**, **37**, 38–39, 43–44, 46, 48, 62, 64, 68–69, **71**, 73, **74**, 77
Führer der Torpedoboote (F.d.T.), Torpedo Boat Leader 6, 14, **15**, 38, 40–41, 52–53, 70–71, 74

German Navy 4, **5**, 7, 17, 34, **76**
    Imperial Navy 6–7, 14, **15**, 35, 39, **49**
    Kriegsmarine 4, **5**, 6–8, **10**, 11–13, **15**, 18–19, **20**, **21**, **24**, 25, **26**, **27**, **28**, 29–30, **33**, 34, **35**, **37**, 39–40, **42**, **43**, **44**, 47–48, **60**, 61–62, 64, **65**, 68, 70–72, **73**, 75, **76**, 77–78
    Reichsmarine 7, 11, **12**, 13–14, **16**, 18, 20, 24–25, 29, **49**
Germany 4–7, **8**, 11–12, **13**, 15–21, 24, **37**, **38**, 42, 47, 48, 53, **57**, 64, 73, 75–78
Göring, Hermann **26**, 27, **43**, 68, 76

harbours 8, **10**, **14**, 29, 34, **35**, 44, 46, **47**, **50**, **56**, **62**, 69–70, **71**, 72–73, 75
Hitler, Adolf **5**, 7, 12, 18, 26–27, **44**, 46, 60, 62, 70–71, 76

Le Havre **21**, **36**, 42, **45**, 47, 70, **71**
London 7–8, 13, 17, 19, **31**, **36**, **45**, 53, **54**, **62**
Luftwaffe 4, 6–8, **26**, **27**, 29, 32–34, 38, **43**, **44**, 47, 49, 52–53, 60–61, **62**, 64, 68–72, 75, 78
Lütjens, *Konteradmiral* Günther 13, **15**, 40, **44**, 52–53, 56, **57**

Marinegruppenkommando (MGK) West 6, 26, 34–35, **37**, 38–41, 43, **44**, 47–49, 60–61, **62**, 68–69, 71, 73–75, **78**
Marschall, *Vizeadmiral* Wilhelm **16**, 49, 60–61, **62**
Marinebefehlshaber, Naval Commander **36**, **37**, 39–40, 44
Marinegruppenkommando (MGK) 6, 26, 34–35, **37**, **38**, 39–41, 43, **44**, 47–49, 60–61, 62, 68–69, 71, 73–75, 78
merchant shipping 5, 7–8, 10, 24, 26–27, 33, 43, 47, 49, 52–54, 61, 69–70, 72, 74–75, 77
minefields 5, **9**, 27, 30, **31**, 43, 53, 56–57, 61, 71, 73–74
minelayers 7, **16**, 33, 40, 48, 54, 56–57, 64, 74
minelaying 7, 14, **16**, 19, **20**, 21, 27, **33**, 40, **42**, 48, **49**, 53–55, **56**, **57**, 60, 69–77
minesweepers 7, **10**, **20**, **21**, **24**, 33–34, 41, 57, 60, 64, 72, 74

Netherlands 10, **35**, **37**, 39–40, 42, 46, 64, **71**, 75
North Sea 4–8, 11, **17**, **19**, **20**, 25–27, 29–30, 35, **36**, **37**, 38, 40–42, **44**, 48, **49**, 52–53, 56, **57**, 60–61, **62**, **71**, **72**, 73, **74**, 75, **76**, 77

Norway 5, 10, 27, 35, 40, **44**, 46–47, **49**, 53, **56**, 61, **62**, 64, **65**, 70, 77

Oberkommando der Kriegsmarine (OKM) 5, 33–34, 43, 56
Operation *Seelöwe* (Sealion) **8**, 10, 35, **44**, 70–71

ports 6, 8, **13**, 24, 34, **35**, 40, 42, 44, **47**, 49, **50**, 52–53, 55–57, 65, 70–71, 74–76, 78

Räumboote (R-boats) 6, **20**, **21**, **24**, 33, **37**, 47, 57, 72–73, **74**
Raeder, *Grossadmiral* Erich **5**, 14, 27, 34, 43, 46, 49, 70, 76
Royal Air Force (RAF) **38**, **44**, 47, 60, **62**, 68, 70, 72–73, 75
Royal Navy 6–7, 18, **21**, 24, 27, 42–43, **44**, 47, 49, 52–54, 60, **62**, 69–70, 72, **73**, 74
    ships 6–7, **21**, 54–56, **57**, **60**, 61, **62**, 64, **65**, 68–69, 74, 77

Saalwächter, *Admiral* Alfred 26–27, 35, **37**, 38–39, **44**, 48–49, 52, 54–55, 57, 60–61, **62**, 71
Schnellboote (S-boats) 6, **9**, 10, **17**, 18, 21, 24, **25**, 28, **29**, 32–33, 38, 41, 44, 46–48, **50**, 52, 64, **65**, 68, 69–71, **72**, 73–77
Seekriegsleitung (SKL) 33–35, 38, 42–43, 49, 52, 57, 60–61, **62**, 68–70, 78
Skagerrak 7, **16**, 35, 49, 52–53, 61

torpedo boats 6–7, 11–13, **16**, 17–20, 24, **26**, **32**, 33, 35, 38, 40–41, **42**, 61, 64, 69, 71–74, 77
    motor torpedo boats (MTB) 20, 24, 46, 69–70, 72, 75, 78
torpedo tubes 14, 17, 19, 25, 28–29, **64**
torpedoes 16–18, **21**, 26–27, **28**, 29, 42, 47, **50**, 52, 55–56, **57**, 60, 64, **65**, 68–69, 72–74, 76–77
Treaty of Versailles 7, 12, 14, 16–18, 20, 24, 76

U-boats 4, 6–7, 12, 16–18, 28, 30, 33, 35, **38**, 47–49, 52, 55–56, 64, **65**, 68, 72, 78
U-Boot Jäger (submarine hunters) **10**, 21, **37**, 47, **60**, 74

Vorpostenboote (patrol boats) **10**, 11, 21, **37**, 42, 47, 52, 61

Wehrmacht 4, 7, **8**, 27, 35, 43, **44**, 70, 75–77
Wilhelmshaven 26, **37**, 41, 44, 52, 55–57, 61, **62**, **63**, 65
World War I 6–7, 12, **13**, 16, 20, 24–25, 28–30, 35, **38**, 41, 49